DEDICATION

I would like to dedicate this book to all Pastors, who fulfill the calling of God through their faithful and diligent service. Without you, our labor would be in vain.

ACKNOWLEDGEMENTS

I would like to thank all the volunteers who generously gave their time and energy to transcribe my messages.

Thank you to my husband Ray, my dear friend Cindy, Nancy, Shellie and Chris—who, as the Shekinah Glory team, worked together to make this book possible.

TABLE OF CONTENTS

FOREWORD

My wife Denise and I have known Lois and Ray Taucher and Cindy Duvall for nearly thirty years at this writing. Their ministry has blessed us so tremendously over the years, and they have been with us through all the major mile-markers of our ministry. Shekinah Glory was there when we dedicated our church in Latvia, and they have ministered several times in our church in Moscow. They don't only preach and teach the Word of God in depth and in power—they impart God's truth and life into us and our congregations.

I have always said that the inspiration I get from just one statement from Lois Taucher can bring forth ten messages! There are some ministers that take license with the Word from time to time, but I have found that *everything* Lois says is soundly based upon Scripture. That's why her teaching always has such a powerful impact.

The book you hold in your hands might be one of the most powerful revelations of the church, and particularly the local church, that you will ever read. I encourage you to read and then re-read this book. Study its contents. Give it to your friends in the Lord and discuss it. Why? Because this is a picture of the body of Christ and the church of the Living God that will change your life forever.

Rick Renner
Moscow Good News Church

FOREWORD

"There comes a special moment in everyone's life, a moment for which that person was born. That special opportunity, when he seizes it, will fulfill his mission—a mission for which he is uniquely qualified. In that moment, he finds greatness. It is his finest hour."

—Winston Churchill

WAKE-UP CALL!

In 2001 we were ministering in a church just outside New York City. We had planned to go into the city during one of the days we were there, which would have put us at the World Trade Center in the early morning of September 11. The night before, after the meeting at the church, we were talking to the pastor and he said, "Well, tomorrow we will take the ferry…," and he went on to tell us how we would see the city the next day.

I said, "You know, Pastor, I don't think I want to go." We had planned this for months, and suddenly I just had no desire to go. The Holy Spirit led us to change our plans after that church meeting, and as a result we avoided a tragic situation that could have cost one or all of us our lives.

The following night, the attacks that had taken place against our country weighed heavily on our hearts. As we were ministering in the same church, I heard God say in my spirit, "Build My Church."

The events of 9-11 changed not only the United States, but nearly every major country in the world. Since that day, leaders have risen and fallen with breakneck speed. Economies have collapsed and men in financial or political power have come to

ruin. One thing has become clear: man's power and position mean absolutely nothing and can change in an instant.

The most powerful people in this world are not the political leaders, the wealthy, or the famous. The most powerful people in this world are believers in Jesus Christ who understand what God is doing on the Earth today.

They understand that being in Christ automatically puts them in God's strategic plan for their time and their hour. As a result, they destroy evil and cause cataclysmic change for good—so good that no secular mind can argue against the results and no lost heart can resist the Lord of those results.

If you have no idea what I am talking about, then I am really glad you picked up this book! This is your wake-up call to renew your understanding of who you are in Jesus Christ—or find out if you don't know—and then discover the life-transforming power of knowing what God is doing today, how He is doing it, and what part He has ordained for you to play in what He's doing.

I can promise you that any depression or oppression, any helplessness or hopelessness, and any aimlessness will lift off of you when you begin to be aware of who you are and what your divine purpose is. Maybe you have a small idea of what it is you are called to do, but it is so much better to see the big picture! Then you can be certain that you are moving in the right direction and that you are not at cross-purposes with what God is trying to accomplish in you, for you, and through you.

You are so important to God! His love for you and desire for you to succeed go far beyond the limits of your imagination. He has a vital role for you to play in His plan for your generation,

and He will move Heaven and Earth to see that you step into that plan and see it through to completion. When you embrace these truths, you, too, will prove to be one of the most powerful people on this planet.

YOU ARE HERE...

As I travel around the world, one thing is very clear: people are confused. I hear, "I wish I could figure out what God is up to. This world is in chaos." I understand how easy it is to get confused if you don't know what the Word of God says about the time in which we are living.

Make no mistake, God is still working in and through His church. The world may appear to be in chaos, and like the people I talk to in my travels, you may be confused about what God is up to, but God isn't confused. He knows exactly what He is doing. And not only does He want to reveal His plan to you, He wants to reveal *your* place in that plan.

It isn't His plan for you to wander aimlessly without focus or real direction. To put this in perspective, it's similar to when I go to an unfamiliar mall or shopping center; the first thing I look for is the map or directory that shows where all the stores are located. When I find the directory, the next thing I look for is that little red

X or dot that says, "You are here." Why do I need to know that? Because if I know where I am and where I have to go, then I can figure out how to get there. The directory is God's Word, and the X that marks your spot is the local church.

YOU ARE NO LONGER A MYSTERY

My task is to bring out in the open and make plain what God, who created all this in the first place, has been doing in secret and behind the scenes all along. Through followers of Jesus like yourselves gathered in churches, this extraordinary plan of God is becoming known and talked about even among the angels!

Ephesians 3:9-10 MSG

When Jesus came to this Earth He knew that His death, burial, and resurrection were going to start a new age, the Church Age. Yet the Bible says that the church was a mystery hidden in the mind of Almighty God. He kept the church and how it would begin a secret; but now that the church is a reality, those who are a part of the body can clearly see what was prophesied in the Old Testament.

I will give you a new heart and put a new spirit within you; I will take the heart of stone out of your flesh and give you a heart of flesh.

Ezekiel 36:26

But the saints of the Most High shall receive the kingdom, and possess the kingdom for ever, even for ever and ever.

Daniel 7:18 JPS

These scriptures talk about the new birth and possessing God's kingdom forever. I don't believe any Old Testament believer understood the full meaning of these verses because God was promising an experience that no human being had ever had. First of all, there was spiritual regeneration and the kingdom of God within our spirits—righteousness, peace, and joy in the Holy Ghost (Romans 14:17). And second, there was God's vision not only of the Messiah coming, dying, and rising from the dead, but multiplying Himself in people on the Earth through the power of His Spirit. All of this—the mystery of the church—was in the heart and mind of God way before the beginning of time.

This means the church was preplanned, and your part in the church was preplanned. God has already been where you are going. He put something in your future that is very strategic and that is what the church is all about.

> **But we speak the wisdom of God in a mystery, the hidden *wisdom* which God ordained before the ages for our glory, which none of the rulers of this age knew; for had they known, they would not have crucified the Lord of glory.**
>
> **1 Corinthians 2:7-8**

Satan had no idea about the church. It was a total mystery to him. All he knew was that God was going to send a deliverer (Genesis 3:15), and his response was to kill anyone who could possibly be that deliverer. If he had figured out the plan of God he would never have orchestrated the death of Jesus. Why? Because after Jesus paid the price for sin and rose from the grave, the Church Age began. The mystery hidden in God was revealed, and

suddenly the devil and all his demons were no longer contending with just *one* Jesus. On the Day of Pentecost alone He multiplied Himself in over 3,000 radical, born-again, Holy-Ghost-empowered saints of God!

The Day of Pentecost was a veritable nightmare for the kingdom of darkness! Jesus had expanded His body at an uncontrollable rate, and the new believers were doing the same signs and wonders He had done. They were preaching the same lie-exposing, devil-defeating, people-liberating Gospel. They were pulling all kinds of mind-renewing and life-transforming revelation out of the Scriptures. They were even taking care of the poor and needy and the widows and orphans.

The nightmare continues for the devil and his kingdom, because the phenomenon that started in the upper room that day with 120 believers is still going strong 2000 years later. And you are a part of this! You are no longer a mystery. Your life and purpose are fully known. You are here…in the church of Jesus Christ.

> No one and nothing can stop the ultimate plan of God, but the devil can stop the plan of God *in you*.

YOU WERE CHOSEN FOR THIS TIME

No one and nothing can stop the ultimate plan of God, but the devil can stop the plan of God *in you*.

Jesus said that Satan is a murderer, a thief, a destroyer, a liar, and the father of all lies (John 10:10, 8:44). Every attack and

strategy he launches against the saints of God has one purpose: to kill, steal the destiny of, or deceive as many saints as he can. And what is all his scheming and destruction about? He wants to keep us from participating in what God is doing on the Earth today.

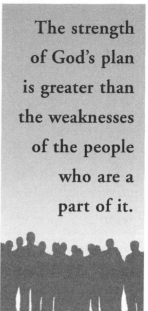

The strength of God's plan is greater than the weaknesses of the people who are a part of it.

God's plan is unchangeable, unconquerable, and indestructible—despite the imperfect people He has to work through! Awareness of what God is doing gives you the ability to see far beyond all your brothers' and sisters' faults, weaknesses, and "issues." **The strength of God's plan is greater than the weaknesses of the people who are a part of it.**

Keeping that focus makes you willing to endure hardship because you know what God is doing on the Earth right now, in your time, and you know that *nothing* can stop His plan from being fulfilled. Remember, you didn't choose the time in which you live, God did.

> **...having definitely determined their allotted periods of time, and the fixed boundaries of their habitation.**
>
> **Acts 17:26** AMP

If you look at any major player in the Bible, you will see that it was their focus on the plan of God for their time that motivated and empowered them to move forward in what God had called them to do, regardless of their circumstances. Moses, for example, had to lead all those "stiff-necked," stubborn, carnal people out of Egypt,

through the Red Sea, around and around in the wilderness for forty years—and yet he kept going. What kept him going? He knew the plan of God for his time, and he was determined to do his part.

Moses had his eyes on the purpose of God. He knew what God had said to him, and that He could and would keep His promise. It didn't matter what the Israelites did—and we know from the Scriptures that there were times when he just threw up his hands and said, "Forget it! These people are impossible!" But he picked himself back up and kept moving forward in faith with his eyes on the plan of God.

> Today, you are also marked by the time in which you are living: You are marked as a member of the body of Jesus Christ.

Moses knew what era he was in and he surrendered his entire life to fulfilling his part in God's plan for that hour. He was marked by God, which meant he was marked by the time in which he was living. Today, you are also marked by the time in which you are living: You are marked as a member of the body of Jesus Christ. The devil knows this, and he will do anything he can to stop you from fulfilling your part in God's plan. But be of good cheer! The gates of Hell will not prevail against the church, and you are a member of the church.

YOU ARE IN THE CHURCH AGE

You are in the Age of the Church, which the Bible reveals is one of seven ages of time that define the entire history of mankind.

Bear with me. I promise I am going to share all seven with you in a couple of pages, but first I need to lay the groundwork.

When a new era begins on God's timeline, that means a new revelation or truth about His purpose and plan has come (Hebrews 1:1).

Each age dispenses a revelation of God and what He is doing in that hour and time. Let's look at this word "dispensation." It is a New Testament word that is often misunderstood.

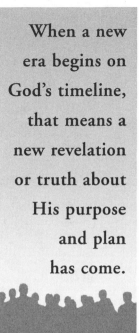

When a new era begins on God's timeline, that means a new revelation or truth about His purpose and plan has come.

For this cause I Paul, the prisoner of Jesus Christ for you Gentiles,

If ye have heard of the *dispensation* of the grace of God which is given me to you-ward:

How that by revelation he made known unto me the mystery; (as I wrote afore in few words,

Whereby, when ye read, ye may understand my knowledge in the mystery of Christ)

Which in other ages was not made known unto the sons of men, as it is now revealed unto his holy apostles and prophets by the Spirit.

Ephesians 3:1-5 KJV (italics mine)

The Greek word translated "dispensation" is *oikonomia,* which means, "1. the management of a household or of household affairs a. specifically, the management, oversight, administration, of

other's property b. the office of a manager or overseer, stewardship c. administration, dispensation."[2] Paul is saying, "My part in God's plan for this hour is to dispense, administrate, manage, and steward the grace of God regarding the mystery of the church.[3] Paul's household was the church of Jesus Christ, to whom he was to dispense the divine purpose of God: the revelation of His grace manifested in His church.

God called Paul to reveal the mystery of the church and how Jesus' body was to operate and function in His grace. Paul and the apostles and disciples of his day knew that when Jesus rose from the dead and filled them with the Holy Ghost on the Day of Pentecost, a new era had begun.

To understand the full weight of the time in which we are living, the Church Age—which is the dispensation of the grace of God—you must know what came before.

THE SEVEN AGES OF MANKIND

1. The Age of Innocence. This era began with the creation of Adam, and it included Adam's and Eve's time in the Garden. They walked and talked with God in complete purity and perfection. The divine purpose of God in this age was His original intent in creating human beings—and it's all good! He created us to love, to bless, to have fellowship, and to be fruitful and multiply. We were designed to worship Him, to be His family, and with Him to steward and enjoy His creation.

2. The Age of Conscience. This era began the moment Adam sinned and he and Eve lost God's glory and presence in their lives.

They became spiritually dead and eternally separated from Him, and that spiritual condition is the root of every problem human beings have had since then. Sin reigned until finally God sent the Flood and began again with Noah and his family. The dispensation of this age was that our conscience knew right from wrong but without God we were unable to keep from sinning.

3. The Age of Human Government. After the Flood, Noah's descendants decided they could get to Heaven by building a tower. Everyone spoke the same language, and they were in complete unity.

> They said, "Come, let us build for ourselves a city, and a tower whose top will reach into heaven, and let us make for ourselves a name, otherwise we will be scattered abroad over the face of the whole earth."
>
> The LORD came down to see the city and the tower which the sons of men had built.
>
> The LORD said, "Behold, they are one people, and they all have the same language. And this is what they began to do, and now nothing which they purpose to do will be impossible for them.
>
> "Come, let Us go down and there confuse their language, so that they will not understand one another's speech."
>
> So the LORD scattered them abroad from there over the face of the whole earth; and they stopped building the city.
>
> **Genesis 11:4-8** NASB

When the Tower of Babel was built the people were in total agreement. There was only one problem: they were not in agreement with God! They weren't serving Him or seeking Him. They were serving themselves and walking in their own understanding.

That is exactly where many people are today. They believe doing right is doing whatever *they think* is right—as though the standard for right and wrong is not determined by God but by how they think and feel about something. This is the ultimate conceit and pride, but God still looked down on these people and dispensed His grace to them by giving them different languages and scattering them throughout the Earth. He gave them another chance to wrestle with their human condition and see that they were sinners in need of a savior.

> Today many people have once again turned from God and look to human government for their problems.

Today many people have once again turned from God and look to human government for answers to their problems. Human government always believes that education alone will unify people and eradicate crime and cruelty in society. This is their tower to Heaven on Earth: If we can all just attain the right knowledge then we will have world peace and tolerance. They make no place for the fallen condition of people and the need for a redeemer who will make a way for them to have a clean heart and be reconciled to God.

The divine truth dispensed during this age was that human government, no matter how unified and successful, does not get you to Heaven or solve your root problem—eternal separation from God because of sin.

4. The Age of the Promise. This era began when God tapped a man named Abraham on the shoulder, took him out of a pagan religion and lifestyle, and gave him a promise—his descendants would be God's beloved people. They would be prosperous, great in number, and live in a land called Canaan. (See Genesis 17:1-8.) Like Noah before him, Abraham understood the time in which he lived because he believed the promise of God. He got the revelation of his time and knew where he fit in the plan of God. Simply put: he had faith that God would keep His promise.

> **Without weakening in his faith, he faced the fact that his body was as good as dead—since he was about a hundred years old—and that Sarah's womb was also dead. Yet he did not waver through unbelief regarding the promise of God, but was strengthened in his faith and gave glory to God, being fully persuaded that God had power to do what he had promised. This is why "it was credited to him as righteousness."**
>
> **Romans 4:19-22 NIV**

Abraham understood what God was doing and he said, "I want to be a part of this. I want to be God's person to bring forth a people for Him, who will live in the land He has destined them to live in, worship Him alone, and be part of His redemptive plan for all people for all ages." The dispensation of Abraham's time was

that God was establishing a nation that would be a blessing to other nations by bringing forth the Redeemer, the "seed of the woman" He promised in Genesis 3:15.

5. **The Age of the Law.** This era was marked by a man named Moses, or you could say that Moses was marked by his time. Abraham's descendants, the children of Israel, had become enslaved in Egypt and needed to be restored to their land and their divine purpose. God used Moses to lead them out of bondage and then gave him the Law. Because God knew they could never keep the Law, He included sacrifices that would cover their sins and teach them that only the shedding of innocent blood could save them from their sins. The Law exposed sin, and the sacrifices spoke of blood being the only atonement for sin. This dispensation of God's divine purpose was that we are sinners in need of a perfect, eternal sacrifice.

> **Every previous age points to the age you and I are in right now!**

There is a pattern here. **Every previous age points to the age you and I are in right now!** We are cursed and suffer because we are eternally separated from God. We have a conscience, but we have no inner strength to do right. No matter how we develop our human abilities, we cannot create Heaven on Earth. We cling to the promise that God will deliver us into a better life and a better place. And finally we see that we are lost in our sins and trespasses, and that only the perfect sacrifice—a sinless blood sacrifice—will save us. All of these dispensations point to Jesus and His church.

6. The Age of the Church. The Age of the Law led right to the sixth dispensation of the divine purpose of God, which is His grace revealed in the church of Jesus Christ. You are living in the time when God is dispensing the full revelation of His grace towards you, in you, and through you. You are marked by this historical event: Jesus died and rose again on the third day to give you a brand new existence in Him—and you are not alone! He has put you in the church, His body, the mystery that has been revealed by his apostles and prophets in the New Testament.

You are probably thinking, *If I am in the sixth age and there are seven, what is the seventh age? What do I have to look forward to in the future?*

7. The Age of Divine Government. This begins when Jesus returns to Earth, throws Satan off the planet, and the kingdoms of this world will become the kingdoms of our God (Revelation 11:15). You will be in your resurrection body, and you will no longer have to contend with your flesh. Hallelujah! But until Jesus returns, you have a lot to do! You are not marked by this coming age yet. You are marked by the dispensation of God's divine purpose in this era: to reveal His grace as a member of the prevailing church of Jesus Christ.

YOU CAN DO YOUR PART

I want to point out that every person God used during these different ages was terribly flawed and often weak. Personally, I don't know if I would have put some of the details about these people in the Bible! But that just underscores the truth that no one

I want to point out that every person God used during these different ages was terribly flawed and often weak.

and nothing can stop the plan of God. All we have to do is to want His plan more than our own selfish plan and follow Jesus.

It is interesting to me that in Hebrews 11:4-39, what we call "The Faith Hall of Fame," there is no mention of all the sins of the children of Israel, their wandering in the wilderness for forty years, or that the older generation never entered the Promised Land because of their unbelief (Hebrews 3:19). The Scripture just goes from them crossing the Red Sea to shouting down the walls of Jericho. Why is that? I believe God wants us to focus on His plan and purpose, which is greater than our faults and failures. He always manages to succeed and carry us through no matter how badly we mess up.

You have to determine to keep your eyes focused on the things of God, on the part He has called you to play in this dispensation of His divine purpose. This focus has always enabled me to look more kindly upon my brothers and sisters and not be so judgmental when one of us sins or does something wrong.

Moses was on the backside of a desert, running scared because he killed an Egyptian guard, when God went and got him. He said, "It is time for you to go back to Egypt and get My people."

Moses said, "I don't think I can do it."

God said, "I don't really care if you don't think you can do it. I didn't ask you how you felt about it. I didn't ask you if you wanted to do it. *Just do it.*" (All the great advertising slogans come from the Word of God!)

I always say God reserves His best for those who leave the choice to Him, and that is what Moses did. He chose God's plan for his time, and he chose to play the part God wanted him to play in his time. You see, your ability to fulfill your calling is dependent upon your understanding of the time you are in and what God wants to accomplish in your time. For instance, God is no longer asking His people to build boats like Noah, or migrate to a new land of promise like Moses and the Israelites. Those days are over. If you understand that in these last days, God is raising you up to function as part of His local church, then you can be assured you will succeed because His plan cannot fail! If He called you and you surrender to that call, then He will make a way for you to fulfill that call and play your part in His plan.

When you're walking by faith like Noah, Abraham, or Moses, you don't always see the big picture. You know the things God has told you by His Spirit and in His Word, and those things are strong enough to get you where He has asked you to go. He did not tell Moses how many times Pharaoh would say no. We know how many times Pharaoh said no because we are on

> I always say God reserves His best for those who leave the choice to Him. Your ability to fulfill your calling is dependent upon your understanding of the time you are in and what God wants to accomplish in your time.

the other side of that part of history. We can read the whole story in the Bible, but Moses walked into Pharaoh's court not knowing exactly how God was going to get this hard-hearted, pagan ruler to let His people go. He only knew that God wanted to deliver His people, and he believed God would use him to get what He wanted.

Moses wasn't listening for the "no." He was listening for the "yes."

Have you heard "no" more than you've heard "yes"? What are you listening for? Are you listening for the "no" or are you listening for the "yes"? Moses looked for the "yes" because God had said "yes," and since God had said "yes," he knew if he didn't quit he was going to get a "yes." Glory!

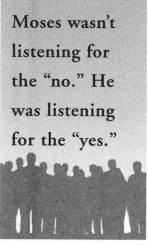

Moses wasn't listening for the "no." He was listening for the "yes."

The significance of Moses' life began the moment he said "yes" to God's plan for his time, and the eternal significance of Moses' life was established because he continued to expect and to listen for God's "yes."

Hebrews 11's Faith Hall of Fame describes the significance of each person's life in just a few sentences, and sometimes just one sentence. Here are some of those who said "yes" to God:

> **By faith Abel offered unto God a more excellent sacrifice than Cain, by which he obtained witness that he was righteous, God testifying of his gifts: and by it he being dead yet speaketh.**

By faith Enoch was translated that he should not see death; and was not found, because God had translated him: for before his translation he had this testimony, that he pleased God.

By faith Noah, being warned of God of things not seen as yet, moved with fear, prepared an ark to the saving of his house; by the which he condemned the world, and became heir of the righteousness which is by faith.

By faith Abraham, when he was called to go out into a place which he should after receive for an inheritance, obeyed; and he went out, not knowing whither he went.

Through faith also Sara herself received strength to conceive seed, and was delivered of a child when she was past age, because she judged him faithful who had promised.

Hebrews 11:4-5,7-8,11,24-26 KJV

I don't know about you, but I read this and am in awe of what these saints of God accomplished in their time for God. I have to remind myself, and I'm reminding you, that they were not any wiser or stronger or more gifted than you or me. We have to remember that God can do through us what He has purposed to do if we will just let Him. It isn't us. It is Him.

It's His plan, and His plan cannot be stopped.

By faith Noah built an ark to save his household. Noah lived six hundred years, and God summed up his life in one sentence— but the power of that sentence! God used Noah to accomplish His divine purpose for that time. Through Noah He preserved the righteous line of mankind while removing the wicked from the

The significance of your life can be summed up in a very few words: what you say yes to God about.

Earth. Noah didn't just build a boat and save his family. He perpetuated the line of human beings that would bring forth the Messiah, Jesus. When Noah said yes to God, he said yes to the redemptive purpose of God for his time and for ours!

In the same way, the significance of your life can be summed up in a very few words: what you say yes to God about. It begins when you say yes to the role God wants you to play in your time, in this Church Age. And the significance of your life is forever established as you continue to say yes—no matter what the challenges, the suffering, the obstacles, or the resistance. Remember, if you are saying no to God, you are saying yes to someone else. Who are you saying yes to?

Like all the saints in the Hebrews 11 Faith Hall of Fame, you can overcome everything through God's supernatural wisdom and strength by simply keeping your focus on His plan and your part in His plan for today. What is His plan for today? The church!

You are here...in the church of Jesus Christ.

2

YOUR DIVINE CONNECTION REVEALS YOUR DIVINE PURPOSE

Ray, and Cindy and I have been working together for more than thirty years at this writing, and we have discovered this truth: Your relationships are just as important as your revelations.

One of the main reasons Shekinah Glory has endured for so many years is because we understand the importance of relationships and we don't burn bridges; we build bridges. Some people disconnect too easily when it gets tough. We have found that the time you feel like you want to disconnect is almost always when you are about to experience a breakthrough.

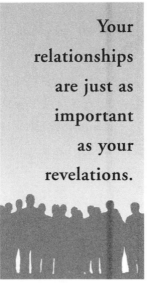

Your relationships are just as important as your revelations.

> **It doesn't really have anything to do with what you want; it has to do with you choosing what God wants.**

It is at this point you choose whether to grow up or not. You are challenged to choose to walk in love, to believe God, to adapt, and to do whatever it takes to preserve the relationship and allow it to grow into something greater than it was. I'm not saying you go against the leading of the Spirit or compromise the Word of God in order to keep a relationship, but you fulfill the parts of the Word that call you to be loving, wise, patient, and full of faith toward your brothers and sisters in Christ.

When someone has hurt you deeply, you may say, "I don't want to forgive and go on!" It doesn't really have anything to do with what you want; it has to do with you choosing what God wants. God always uses people to get you where you need to go and to get you to grow up spiritually. When you accept the principle that your relationships are just as important as your revelations, you will make more progress than you would alone.

You will never be the person He has created you to be or accomplish all He has called you to do by yourself. For you to fulfill your divine purpose in your time, you must understand the great plan that God has made you a part of. You are in the church. If you are born again, then you are a part of God's family and Christ's body. You are a member of the body of Jesus Christ.

Being a member of the body of Christ is not like joining a country club; it's about having fellowship with the saints God has put you in relationship with. Fellowship makes relationships real, because fellowship is more than greeting someone at the door. Fellowship is working in ministry with other believers to make disciples, and that kind of fellowship requires you to develop spiritual maturity. It requires you to look beyond yourself and your own needs and desires and consider the needs and desires of others. It also provides opportunities for you to discover and use the gifts God has given you and move into what He has called you to do and to give.

For you to fulfill your divine purpose in your time, you must understand the great plan that God has made you a part of. You are in the church.

If you are not in fellowship with the people of God, then your place in the body of Christ will not be real or important to you. Because you are not doing your part in a church family, you cannot see or understand your contribution to the body of Christ at large. You may not realize it, but not participating in a church causes you to live for yourself and not for the plan of God. Why? Jesus died for the church! He is building the church right now. If you aren't in church, you aren't in the place He has for you; and if you aren't in your place you cannot do your part.

Believers who go to church only when they feel like it really don't get the big picture. I've seen it happen many times – they gradually stop giving of their time, their gifts, and their finances. Bible study and prayer times are few and far between. Eventually,

they quit going to church at all, and without the influence of a Pastor and church family, they may even stop believing altogether. And if you'll remember, unbelief is what kept the older generation of the children of Israel out of the Promised Land (Hebrews 3:19). Separated from the body of Christ, their commitment to Jesus and His church hangs by a thread – it's a dangerous place to be.

I heard on the news one day that the reason so many military service men and women re-enlist today is because they are trained and deployed as units, they do not want to be separated. This is in contrast to the Vietnam War, when service people were deployed as individuals instead of units, and there were fewer re-enlistments. Back then young men were drafted; today we have a volunteer military and more re-enlistments. I believe it is because the military understands the importance of being a member of a group. Each soldier is trained for and assigned individual tasks, but they function together to reach a common goal: defeat the enemy.

> **The way you view God's people reveals the way you view God.**

When I heard that report I thought, *That's what happens when you understand you are a member of the body of Christ. You don't go AWOL because you're not going into battle alone. You're going as a unit.* Someone once said that the church is not a cruise ship; it's a battleship. It's where you grow deeply anchored in God's Word and everyone does their part because all their lives depend on it. That kind of commitment makes it an honor to lay your life down for your brothers and sisters.

The way you view God's people reveals the way you view God. God loves His people and He wants you to love them too. He created you to be a part of a family and a member of a body. Those are both very intimate relationships, and those relationships happen to be the key to your understanding who you are and where you fit into God's strategic plan for today: the church.

A CALLED-OUT ASSEMBLY

The significance and power of your place in God's family, Christ's body, and the local church is revealed even more when you understand the meaning of the word that was translated "church." Why did Jesus—and the Holy Spirit—choose this particular word?

Jesus was the first to use the word "church" in Matthew 16:18, when He said He would build His church. The Greek word for church is *ekklesia,* and this word is used 114 times in the New Testament. Ninety of those references refer to a local assembly of believers. The reason I tell you this is that sometimes believers don't want to emphasize the local church. They just want to talk about the universal church. They believe you don't really need to have a pastor in your life or a place where you come together with the same group of saints on a regular basis. They can just go to a coffee shop and talk about Jesus with a couple of friends and have "church."

> Jesus was the first to use the word "church" in Matthew 16:18, when He said He would build His church.

Everything God is doing today, He is doing through the *local* church.

Getting together with a couple of Christian friends is not having church. It is good, but it is not the same. Believers are beginning to have all kinds of unscriptural ideas about the local church and the universal church, and because of this thinking they are diminishing the work of God and losing sight of the plan of God.

Who did Jesus say would bind and loose? "My church." Who did Jesus say would prevail against the gates of Hell? "My church." So let's find out exactly what His church is—what the church of Jesus is supposed to look like, act like, and sound like.

The word *ekklesia* literally means, "a called-out assembly."[1] We are right back to relationships! First of all, we have to have a relationship with the One who calls us out; then we have relationships with the ones with whom He calls us to assemble. The One who calls us to assemble gives us His strategic plan *when we are assembled.* Assembly is required!

The church is not just a group of people who have decided to meet on a regular basis. The church is a group of people who have heard the call of God and have come together under the unction and anointing of the Holy Ghost. You may not *know* why you're there, but that's why you're there! You are not meeting with a group so that God can be a part of

Assembly is required!

your plan; He has brought you together to be a part of His plan!

God is the one who calls you out to assemble with other saints in the local church. Then, as you are assembled and relating to one another, He reveals your individual purposes in context of your corporate purpose.

> To the church of God which is at Corinth, to those who are sanctified in Christ Jesus, called *to be* saints, with all who in every place call on the name of Jesus Christ our Lord, both theirs and ours.
>
> 1 Corinthians 1:2

In this verse the Greek wording denotes a fixed position in a place, a time, or a state. Again, most of the time in the New Testament, the word church is referring to a local church, not the universal church. As a secular term in the Greek language, *ekklesia* described an assembly of citizens that governed a city or a district. I like William Barclay's definition:

> *Ekklesia* is the NT word for 'church,' and is, therefore, one of the most important of all NT words.
>
> …In the classical days in Athens the *ekklesia* was the convened assembly of the people. This assembly consisted of all the citizens living in the city who had not lost their civic rights. Apart from the fact that its

You are not meeting with a group so that God can be a part of your plan; He has brought you together to be a part of His plan!

> Most of the time in the New Testament, the word church is referring to a local church not the universal church.

decisions must conform to the laws of the State, the assembly's powers were for all intents and purposes unlimited. It elected and dismissed magistrates and directed the policy of the city. It declared war, made peace, contracted treaties, and arranged alliances. It elected generals and other military officers. It assigned troops to different campaigns and dispatched them from the city. It was ultimately responsible for the conduct of all military operations. It raised and allocated funds…. To Greek and Roman alike the word was familiar in the sense of a convened assembly. So, then, when we look at the assembly against this background…the Church was God's assembly…and the convener is God.[2]

Barclay also explains the Hebrew background for the word *ekklesia*:

> The Septuagint (the Greek translation of the Old Testament) translates the Hebrew word *qahal,* which again comes from a root meaning 'to summon.' It is regularly used for the 'assembly' or the 'congregation' of the people of Israel…. In the Hebrew sense it, therefore, means God's people called together by God, in order to listen to or to act for God.

...It means a body of people who have been 'summoned out' of their homes to come and meet with God...a summons from God to every man to come and to listen to and to act on the Word of God.

In essence, therefore, the Church, the *ekklesia*, is a body of people, not so much assembling because they have chosen to come together but assembling because God has called them to himself; not so much assembling to share their own thoughts and opinions, but assembling to listen to the voice of God.[3]

The focus of these definitions of the church is that God calls His people to come together to hear from Him and act on His Word. Since we have established that an *ekklesia* is a particular group called together by God at a particular place, we can deduce what Jesus meant when He used that word. Not only did Jesus declare His goal of building His church, but by choosing *ekklesia* He declared the strategy He would use to build it: the local assembly. It's the local church that reveals the universal church. Without local churches, there is no understanding of the universal church.

> An *ekklesia* is a particular group called together by God at a particular place. It's the local church that reveals the universal church. As part of a local church, you will be supernaturally empowered to play your part in His plan.

I wrote earlier that 90 of the 114 times the word *ekklesia* is used, it refers to a local assembly. While you are living and breathing on planet Earth, you need to be a part of a local church. As part of a local church, you will hear the plan of God and be supernaturally empowered to play your part in His plan. Jesus said, "I will build my *ekklesia,* My convened assembly of people, my elected officials (elected by Me), those I have endowed with power from the Holy Ghost; and the gates of Hell shall not prevail against it."

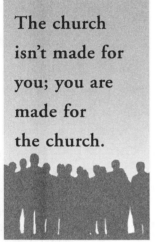

The church isn't made for you; you are made for the church.

THE PLACE OF REVELATION

You must understand that when you become a Christian, the church isn't made for you; you are made for the church. The church is your place in the plan of God! That's where your gifts and calling and knowledge of what it means to be a Christian are revealed. You don't even know what it means to be a Christian until you are in your place in a local assembly. Relationships are the key to all revelation, whether it is concerning the Word or what you are to do today.

I liken it to a jigsaw puzzle, which has a lot of pieces. You pick up a piece that you know belongs in that puzzle, but because certain other pieces are not yet in their places, it is difficult to connect the piece in your hand. It is hard to see the full meaning and purpose of that piece until it is properly connected with the other pieces. It is an essential part, but its effectiveness is greatly diminished unless it is connected. You know that it is significant, and its color and sometimes its shape can give you an idea where it goes; so you don't want to set it aside or lose it.

Sometimes you don't know the piece is missing until you need it! By then it can be too late. You put the piece somewhere and don't remember where it is. The piece is not where it is supposed to be, in the company of the pieces it connects to. It is gone, so there is no hope of it realizing its destiny. But I want to encourage you, it might be too late with a puzzle piece, but thank God it is not too late for you! You are still breathing. You are still His beloved child. Find your place in His local church. You may be the piece that completes the puzzle by reaching your neighborhood, going on a mission trip, or even bringing Jesus back!

> Believers who just look at themselves without connecting to the local church are like people who hold one puzzle piece in their hands and never connect it.

Believers who just look at themselves without connecting to the local church are like people who hold one puzzle piece in their hands and never connect it. All they know is what's on that piece. They don't see the whole picture, and they will never know the fullness of their identity and purpose because they don't see themselves through God's eyes: in context of the whole body. They don't see what God is doing in their place and time. All they

You have to play your part in the big picture to see and understand the big picture.

see is their one little piece, which doesn't tell them much.

At the other end of the spectrum are the believers who try to make themselves fit into places they were never created to fit. They also end up never knowing their full potential and all the joys and blessings God has for them. They are not connected properly. That's why relationships need to be established by God. It is *divine* connections that enable us to fulfill our divine purpose.

The local church is the place of God's assembly, so you must start with the place where He has called you. Then you will better understand your time and you can do your part. If you miss your place you will never understand the strategic plan of God. You will never see the big picture, and your ability to grow in revelation will be hindered. You have to play your part in the big picture to see and understand the big picture. So the first thing you must do is ask the Lord, "Where is my church? Where is the assembly of believers You are calling me to?"

BARNABAS THE ENCOURAGER

The Bible is full of examples of how important it is to connect with the local church. Every person who played a significant role in the plan of God, functioning throughout the epistles and the book of Acts, had a part in a local church. They knew they could not do their part if they were not in their place, divinely connected for their divine purpose. Barnabas was a great example of this. The first time we hear of him is in Acts, chapter 4, where we also find out the significance of his name.

> **And Joses, who was also named Barnabas by the apostles (which is translated Son of Encouragement), a Levite of the country of Cyprus, having land, sold *it,* and brought the money and laid *it* at the apostles' feet.**
>
> Acts 4:36-37

A man named Joses lived on the island of Cyprus. He was a Levite, who was probably in Jerusalem on the Day of Pentecost and had been saved and filled with the Holy Ghost. He sold some land and brought the money he made to the apostles, and they were so

> *Every person who played a significant role in the plan of God, functioning throughout the Epistles and the book of Acts, had a part in a local church.*

encouraged by what he did that they changed his name to Barnabas, which means, "Son of Encouragement." This man's whole life was an encouragement to the local church first and therefore the church at large.

The greatest thing you can do to facilitate the work of God is to be an encouragement to your local church. Sometimes when there is a great need in a church, people think, *Well, there must be something wrong with the pastors. Why haven't they done something about this?* But Barnabas didn't think that way. He saw the need

The greatest thing you can do to facilitate the work of God is to be an encouragement to your local church.

and thought, *What can I do to help make this happen?* Great things get done when the people of God realize that Jesus wants to use *them* to build His church.

We know who Barnabas is today because he said, "What can I do to help build the church in Jerusalem?" He encouraged and financially supported the leadership and the saints there. By the leading of the Holy Spirit he connected with them in relationship and in vision, and as a result he came into his divine purpose. As he was willing to give his life to the call of God in His church, the gifts of God began to flow through him; and the Bible tells us he became one of the great apostles of his day.

In Acts 9:27 Barnabas was the one who brought Saul of Tarsus to the church in Jerusalem. Saul had been on his way to Damascus, where he had planned to arrest some Christians, but Jesus knocked him to the ground and blinded him just long enough to get him to see who He was. Then He sent a disciple named Ananias to lay hands on Saul so that he might be filled with the Holy Ghost and receive his sight.

Do you see how God works? He works through His people! He works in the context of local bodies of believers—the "whosoever wills" like you and me. Ananias and Barnabas were those who were willing to make a divine connection with a person who had persecuted and killed Christians for years. They couldn't have known at the time, but this "divine connection" just happened to be called by God to reveal the mystery of what they were a part of—the church! Their divine connection with Saul of Tarsus, who became the Apostle Paul, was also a key to their divine purpose as part of the church.

Barnabas had made his divine connection with Saul of Tarsus after Saul traveled to Jerusalem to connect with the saints there.

> **Their divine connection with Saul of Tarsus, who became the Apostle Paul, was also a key to their divine purpose as part of the church.**

> **And when Saul had come to Jerusalem, he tried to join the disciples; but they were all afraid of him, and did not believe that he was a disciple. But Barnabas took him and brought *him* to the apostles. And he declared to them how he had seen the Lord on the road, and that He had spoken to him, and how he had preached boldly at Damascus in the name of Jesus. So he was with them at Jerusalem, coming in and going out.**
>
> **Acts 9:26-28**

Barnabas was just a believer being an encouragement to the church in Jerusalem, but God strategically used him to bring under the leadership of the local church one of the most important apostles and prophets in church history. Barnabas knew that the key to this new convert's success was to be connected to a local body of believers. He just happened to be the man whom the Holy

Spirit would use to write most of the New Testament! Paul would reveal the mystery of the church, the grace of God, our redemption in Jesus Christ through His sinless blood and consequent resurrection, our freedom from sin and new life in Him, and all the facets of our life in Christ now and forever.

ESTABLISHING A LOCAL ASSEMBLY

In Acts, chapter 11, we still find Barnabas being an encouragement to the church at Jerusalem. He has become a trusted member of that body of believers, and the leaders decided to send him out on a special mission.

> Barnabas knew that the only way these new converts would keep the faith for the rest of their lives was to establish them as a local assembly, an *ekklesia.*

Now those who were scattered after the persecution that arose over Stephen traveled as far as Phoenicia, Cyprus, and Antioch, preaching the word to no one but the Jews only. But some of them were men from Cyprus and Cyrene, who, when they had come to Antioch, spoke to the Hellenists, preaching the Lord Jesus. And the hand of the Lord was with them, and a great number believed and turned to the Lord.

Then news of these things came to the ears of the church in Jerusalem, and they sent out Barnabas to go as far as Antioch. When he came and had seen the grace of God, he was glad, and encouraged them all that with purpose of heart they should continue with the Lord. For he was a good man, full of the Holy Spirit and of faith. And a great many people were added to the Lord.

Acts 11:19-24

When Barnabas came to Antioch he saw the grace of God and was glad. *The Message* says, "As soon as he arrived, he saw that God was behind it and in it. He threw himself in with them, got behind them, urging them to stay with it the rest of their lives." Now, how were they going to stay with it the rest of their lives? Look at what Barnabas did next.

Then Barnabas departed for Tarsus to seek Saul. And when he had found him, he brought him to Antioch. So it was that for a whole year they assembled with the church and taught a great many people. And the disciples were first called Christians in Antioch.

Acts 11:25-26

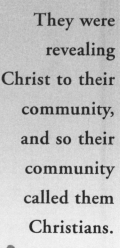

They were revealing Christ to their community, and so their community called them Christians.

Barnabas knew that the only way these new converts would keep the faith for the rest of their lives was to establish them as a local assembly, an *ekklesia*. The Holy Spirit told him, "Go get Saul," which he did. Then, for a whole year Barnabas and Saul "assembled with the church," teaching them the revelation of the church and who they were in Christ Jesus.

Antioch was the first place the disciples were called Christians. What was happening? The plan of God was being unveiled. The saints were being established in their faith, their gifts, and the calling of God. They were revealing Christ to their community, and so their community called them Christians.

What did Saul of Tarsus teach the church in Antioch? We know what he taught through his first letter to the Corinthians.

> **For this reason I have sent Timothy to you, who is my beloved and faithful son in the Lord, who will *remind you of my ways in Christ, as I teach everywhere in every church.***
>
> 1 Corinthians 4:17 (italics mine)

The Apostle Paul taught every church—all the local churches he encouraged in the faith—his ways in Christ. He also lived in front of them what he taught. God had given him a revelation of how the death and resurrection of Jesus Christ had produced the church, which was the manifested presence of the power and glory of God on his people for that hour. God put His power on His people to decimate all the power of darkness as they lifted up Jesus Christ and lived in His way, His truth, and His life.

You say, "This is big stuff! You mean God is just going to use people like me?"

When you gather together in the name of Jesus with the very same power that raised Him from the dead, you are in position to manifest His glorious victory to your generation.

That's right! When you gather together in the name of Jesus with the very same power that raised Him from the dead, you are in position to manifest His glorious victory to your generation. Demons will flee and the blind will see. Darkness will be swallowed up in the glorious life and power of God as the saints gather in local churches all over this world.

THE KEY TO EVERYTHING

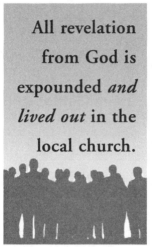

All revelation from God is expounded *and* lived out in the local church.

All revelation from God is expounded *and lived out* in the local church. He convenes us to reveal Himself and His plan to us. If we diminish the place of our local church, we diminish and thwart the plan of God not only for ourselves, but also for our neighborhood, our city, and possibly our region, nation, or the world. If we do not allow the Holy Spirit to connect us properly in a local body of believers, we will never be stirred and provoked and inspired to grow up spiritually, develop our gifts, and fulfill the plan of God for our lives. We will never play our part in His plan.

And let us consider one another in order to stir up love and good works, not forsaking the assembling of ourselves together, as *is* the manner of some, but exhorting *one another,* and so much the more as you see the Day approaching.

Hebrews 10:24-25

Do not neglect or avoid worshipping together! Do not break the habit of meeting together to share your lives in Him and learn of Him. I like how the *New International Version* translates these verses. It says, "Let us not give up meeting together, as some are in the habit of doing, but let us encourage one another—and all the more as you see the day approaching." Encourage one another! No believer's life is without difficulties and challenges. We need each other. We need a family of believers to sustain us in hard times and stir us up and spur us on in good times.

Those who sit at home watching Christian television, sending their tithes and offerings to a televangelist, don't get the kind of encouragement I'm talking about. Their absence from the local church causes the work of God to be greatly hindered. They are a missing piece God needs to complete His big picture.

You say, "What about the handicapped and the elderly, who can't get to church?" Even those who are physically unable to attend a church can be connected to one through regular home visitation—and not just by the pastor. Bible study with the saints, CDs of the messages, and other things connect people to a local church. It's time we got creative about this! A lot of local churches have ministries that include people who cannot get to their services but are an integral part of their congregation. You would be surprised at what these saints of God can contribute. If the key to everything is the local church, then every believer needs to be a part of a local assembly.

Habakkuk 2:14 says that the whole Earth will be filled with the knowledge of His glory. How do you think He is going to do that? He has a very strategic plan for filling the Earth with His glory, and He reveals that strategic plan in Ephesians 3:21 (bold mine), "To Him *be* glory **in the church** by Christ Jesus to all generations, forever and ever." The knowledge and revelation of the glory of God reside and manifest in the church—so be there!

PETER GOT IT AND PAUL REVEALED IT

Jesus walked upon this earth knowing that time was about to change. He knew that by His death, burial, and resurrection a new age would begin—the Church Age. The Church Age was going to be a time when the power that raised Him from the dead would be put on display so all the world could see what God did through Him, and they would see it through His church. The church would be His witness to their generation.

One day Jesus decided it was time to tell His disciples what God was about to do. He began by asking them a question.

> When Jesus came into the region of Caesarea Philippi, He asked His disciples, saying, "Who do men say that I, the Son of Man, am?"
>
> So they said, "Some *say* John the Baptist, some Elijah, and others Jeremiah or one of the prophets."
>
> He said to them, "But who do you say that I am?"

Simon Peter answered and said, "You are the Christ, the Son of the living God."

Jesus answered and said to him, "Blessed are you, Simon Bar-Jonah, for flesh and blood has not revealed *this* to you, but My Father who is in heaven. And I also say to you that you are Peter, and on this rock I will build My church, and the gates of Hades shall not prevail against it. And I will give you the keys of the kingdom of heaven, and whatever you bind on earth will be bound in heaven, and whatever you loose on earth will be loosed in heaven."

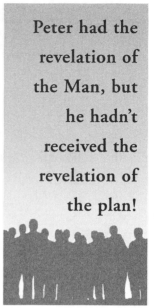

Peter had the revelation of the Man, but he hadn't received the revelation of the plan!

Matthew 16:13-19

Peter received the revelation of who Jesus was, but he had no idea that Jesus was giving him a preview of what would change him from being a self-promoting, unstable coward to a great and humble leader of strength and courage—the church. What happened next indicates that he had no clue.

From that time Jesus began to show to His disciples that He must go to Jerusalem, and suffer many things from the elders and chief priests and scribes, and be killed, and be raised the third day.

Then Peter took Him aside and began to rebuke Him, saying, "Far be it from You, Lord; this shall not happen to You!"

> But He turned and said to Peter, "Get behind Me, Satan! You are an offense to Me, for you are not mindful of the things of God, but the things of men."
>
> Matthew 16:21-23

Peter had the revelation of the Man, but he hadn't received the revelation of the plan! The church was still a mystery to him and the other disciples. They were thinking in terms of people, "mindful of...the things of men," and figured Jesus was going to defeat the Romans and set up His kingdom as a political leader on Earth. They could not conceive that the kingdom of God was a spiritual kingdom through which He would govern the hearts of those who believed in Him. They *really* couldn't conceive of them being in Him and Him being in them!

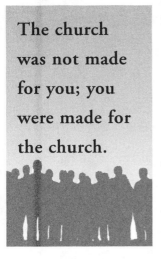

The church was not made for you; you were made for the church.

Then, of course, we know what happened. Jesus was arrested, Peter denied Him three times, Jesus was crucified, all the disciples but John and some of the women fled for their lives, and on the third day—just like He said—Jesus was resurrected from the dead. Peter and John ran to the tomb and found it empty, and then Jesus appeared to them several times. The last time He appeared to them in the book of John, Jesus tried again to explain to Peter what His death and resurrection had set in motion.

> So when they had eaten breakfast, Jesus said to Simon Peter, "Simon, *son* of Jonah, do you love Me more than these?"

He said to Him, "Yes, Lord; You know that I love You."

He said to him, "Feed My lambs."

He said to him again a second time, "Simon, *son* of Jonah, do you love Me?"

He said to Him, "Yes, Lord; You know that I love You."

He said to him, "Tend My sheep."

He said to him the third time, "Simon, *son* of Jonah, do you love Me?" Peter was grieved because He said to him the third time, "Do you love Me?"

And he said to Him, "Lord, You know all things; You know that I love You."

Jesus said to him, "Feed My sheep."

John 21:15-17

Jesus was talking to Peter about his future as a pastor, helping him to understand the truth that the way you treat His people—His sheep—will reveal the way you love Him. Remember: The church was not made for you; you were made for the church.

How did Peter finally get this? When many others left, he remained in the Upper Room. He stayed with the local assembly of believers, and when the Day of Pentecost arrived and the Spirit of God fell on them with tongues of fire on their heads and all kinds of languages coming out of their mouths, Peter was there to receive it. He got it: We, the Lord's body, inhabited by His Spirit, now represent and reveal Jesus to the people of the world.

Although the Apostle Paul was the one to deliver the Word of God on the mystery of the church, Peter was the first to preach a

gospel message. What he had been slow to see in Matthew 16, he had now become by the death, burial and resurrection of Jesus Christ.

"This Jesus God has raised up, of which we are all witnesses. Therefore being exalted to the right hand of God, and having received from the Father the promise of the Holy Spirit, He poured out this which you now see and hear.

"Therefore let all the house of Israel know assuredly that God has made this Jesus, whom you crucified, both Lord and Christ."

Now when they heard *this,* they were cut to the heart, and said to Peter and the rest of the apostles, "Men *and* brethren, what shall we do?"

Then Peter said to them, "Repent, and let every one of you be baptized in the name of Jesus Christ for the remission of sins; and you shall receive the gift of the Holy Spirit. For the promise is to you and to your children, and to all who are afar off, as many as the Lord our God will call."

Acts 2:32-33,36-39

Finally Peter knew what the hope and promise were! The new birth, being reconciled to God through the sinless blood of Jesus, receiving forgiveness of sin, the indwelling and empowerment of the Holy Spirit—all of these incredible blessings brought forth the strategic plan of God for this time: the church. This wasn't a physical, political kingdom. This was a spiritual kingdom that all those ungodly, political world systems and governments could not prevail against!

Peter now understood what Jesus had been saying. "Heaven will open to you when I am raised on the third day, and I will build My church to demonstrate and proclaim My Gospel." How are the lost going to see who God is, how He loves them, what He's doing, His way of life, and His life-giving power and kingdom? They will see Him through the functioning of His church, which is not man-made. It is not people operating in their own ability and reasoning. The church is supernaturally built by Jesus upon the revelation that He is the Messiah, the Son of the Living God.

Just by believing in the resurrection and confessing that Jesus is now Lord of their lives (Romans 10:9-10), on the Day of Pentecost people who were cowards, weak, selfish, violent, and bitter were spiritually transformed into a people who embraced the world with God's love and power. They were miraculously changed by the dynamics of redemption offered through the blood of Jesus. The church was then and still is the place of miraculous and ongoing people-transformation!

> The church was then and still is the place of miraculous and ongoing people-transformation!

Peter finally understood what He had been telling him for three years! Receiving the revelation of Jesus as the Son of God and Head of His church and body was what Peter was created for—it's what *every* Christian was created for!

REVELATION BEGINS
WITH A QUESTION

The question that revealed Jesus as the Messiah and Son of God to Peter was, "Who do you say that I am?" The question that set Peter on the path of building the church was, "Peter, do you love Me?" Then Jesus set another man's heart on fire for God with another unusual question: "Why are you persecuting Me?"

> **Then Saul, still breathing threats and murder against the disciples of the Lord, went to the high priest and asked letters from him to the synagogues of Damascus, so that if he found any who were of the Way, whether men or women, he might bring them bound to Jerusalem.**
>
> **As he journeyed he came near Damascus, and suddenly a light shone around him from heaven. Then he fell to the ground, and heard a voice saying to him, "Saul, Saul, why are you persecuting Me?"**
>
> **And he said, "Who are You, Lord?"**
>
> **Then the Lord said, "I am Jesus, whom you are persecuting. It is hard for you to kick against the goads."**
>
> **So he, trembling and astonished, said, "Lord, what do You want me to do?"**
>
> **Then the Lord *said* to him, "Arise and go into the city, and you will be told what you must do."**
>
> Acts 9:1-6

Saul had an extraordinary experience with Jesus. He saw the light shine out of Heaven, which caused him to fall to the ground. Then he heard the audible voice of Jesus. You may never have heard the audible voice of Jesus, but I will tell you this: You can hear the voice of the Lord so clearly that it is more real than most of the audible voices you hear! He can speak to you in a life-changing way through His Word, by the unction and witness of His Spirit, and through the saints in the church He sends to impart into your life.

However, Jesus dealt with Saul in a striking, supernatural way to get his full attention. He knocked him to the ground with all His glory and asked him a simple question, "Saul, Saul why are you persecuting Me?"

Now Saul was one of the most intelligent and well-educated men of his time, and he was a thinker. He didn't just accept something without looking at it closely and making sure he really understood it. He probably thought, *Persecuting You, Lord?* His mind was reeling, trying to figure out how he could be persecuting the Lord of Glory, so he decided to make sure this really was the Lord of Glory. He said, " Who are You, Lord?"

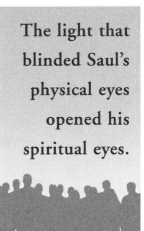

The light that blinded Saul's physical eyes opened his spiritual eyes.

Then Jesus laid it all out clear and simple for him. He said, "I'm Jesus, and you are persecuting *Me.*"

The Bible says Paul was blinded by a heavenly light, and Jesus did that for a reason. The light that blinded Saul's physical eyes opened his spiritual eyes. Saul began to see the truth and thought, *Persecuting Christians is the same as persecuting Jesus. When I persecute, torture, and kill them, He sees that as persecuting, torturing, and killing Him.*

To Him, it's all about His church, and whatever I do to them I do to Him. It's like they are His literal body. Wow! God and people are one through Him.

The Bible says Saul was trembling and astonished, and I believe that was because Jesus had just destroyed his whole understanding of God and his religion. All he could say was, "Lord, what do You want me to do?" Jesus told Saul to go into Damascus, and he would get further instructions there. Jesus was about to demonstrate the revelation Paul had just had by sending a member of His body to minister to him.

THE PERSECUTED MINISTERS TO THE PERSECUTOR

Maybe Saul had heard about Jesus dying on the Cross and crying, "Father, forgive them, for they do not know what they do" (Luke 23:34). Now he was going to experience that divine forgiveness himself—through the ministry of one of the saints. Ananias showed love and forgiveness to him, and that was not business as usual for Saul of Tarsus!

> **Now there was a certain disciple at Damascus named Ananias; and to him the Lord said in a vision, "Ananias."**
>
> **And he said, "Here I am, Lord."**
>
> **So the Lord *said* to him, "Arise and go to the street called Straight, and inquire at the house of Judas for *one* called Saul of Tarsus, for behold, he is praying. And in a vision he has seen a man named Ananias coming in**

and putting *his* hand on him, so that he might receive his sight."

Then Ananias answered, "Lord, I have heard from many about this man, how much harm he has done to Your saints in Jerusalem. And here he has authority from the chief priests to bind all who call on Your name."

But the Lord said to him, "Go, for he is a chosen vessel of Mine to bear My name before Gentiles, kings, and the children of Israel. For I will show him how many things he must suffer for My name's sake."

And Ananias went his way and entered the house; and laying his hands on him he said, "Brother Saul, the Lord Jesus, who appeared to you on the road as you came, has sent me that you may receive your sight and be filled with the Holy Spirit." Immediately there fell from his eyes *something* like scales, and he received his sight at once; and he arose and was baptized.

Acts 9:10-18

> Even the man who was destined to become the great Apostle Paul needed someone in the church, a disciple of the Lord Jesus, to be in position for the call to minister to him.

Even the man who was destined to become the great Apostle Paul needed someone in the church, a disciple of the Lord Jesus, to be in position for the call to minister to him. Nobody is called alone! The

You will never be what God wants you to be until you do what He wants you to do!

call of God is not an individual calling; it's a corporate calling. It's on the church. Paul saw this truth in action from the moment he was saved.

At first Ananias was afraid of Saul and didn't want to go near him. He probably had Christian friends and relatives who had been persecuted or even killed because of Saul, but he did it anyway for Jesus. You will never be what God wants you to be until you do what He wants you to do! I believe when Ananias obeyed, the courage and compassion of the Lord came all over him to minister to Saul.

Ananias laid hands on him, the power of the Holy Spirit hit that old Pharisee, and Saul could see again—but now things looked

None of the writers of the New Testament call the church the body of Christ except Paul.

entirely different! Saul of Tarsus went from "breathing threats and murder against the disciples of the Lord" to receiving a miracle from one of them. That is the church—Jesus' body doing the works that He did (John 14:12)—but doing greater works because there are more of us!

From the moment Saul was saved, he saw Jesus and His church as one. Do you know that none of the writers of the New Testament call the church the body of Christ except Paul? Only Paul calls us the Lord's body because from the moment he found out who he was really persecuting—that when you hurt the church you hurt Jesus—his entire life and identity were marked and directed by the revelation of the mystery of the church: Christ in us, the hope of glory (Colossians 1:27).

When you truly have a revelation of Jesus Christ, you have a revelation of His church. If you don't see the significance of the church, you don't have the revelation of who Jesus is and what He accomplished when He died and rose again. This was the revelation God called Paul to steward.

> **When you truly have a revelation of Jesus Christ, you have a revelation of His church.**

PAUL'S STEWARDSHIP

I now rejoice in my sufferings for you, and fill up in my flesh what is lacking in the afflictions of Christ, for the sake of His body, which is the church, of which I became a minister according to the stewardship from God which was given to me for you, to fulfill the word of God, the mystery which has been hidden from ages and from generations, but now has been revealed to His saints.

Colossians 1:24-26

Paul said that all he suffered was for the church, for the sake of the body of Christ. He said God had given him a stewardship, which speaks of the dispensation or management of the divine purpose of God in his time: the grace of God and the mystery of

Paul's focus remained on strengthening the church, and no amount of suffering or resistance could stop him.

the church. What had been hidden for ages past was now revealed to the saints, and God commissioned Paul to fulfill the Holy Scriptures with the revelation of the church.

Have you ever wondered why some people cannot be stopped while others can be stopped so easily? I think it has a lot to do with their focus. Paul's focus remained on strengthening the church, and no amount of suffering or resistance could stop him.

Weymouth's translation of Colossians 1:25 says, "I have been appointed to serve the Church in the position of responsibility entrusted to me by God for your benefit, so that I may fully deliver God's Message." Paul did not see himself as someone who was doing his own thing. He had gifts and he stood in an office for one purpose: building up the church.

Again, no one else calls the church the body of Christ except Paul. He understood that the church was the functioning body of all Jesus Christ bought and paid for with His blood. He knew the church was not a man-made, secular crowd, but it was the body of the living Jesus Christ exhibited on this Earth. Christians reveal the King of kings and Lord of lords by walking in and demonstrating the freedom and authority given them through His death and resurrection.

It is impossible for secular society or unbelievers to understand the church. To the world, "church" conjures up the image of a building. However, it is possible for them to see the real church whether they comprehend what they are seeing or not. How? In the people who assemble in those buildings— people being transformed and healed by the power of God.

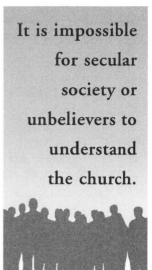

It is impossible for secular society or unbelievers to understand the church.

Paul probably understood the function of the church as being Jesus on the Earth more than anyone else because that was what he encountered both on the road to Damascus and with Ananias in Damascus. Paul also understood how the unsaved mind worked, how the unbeliever thought. He had been in the secular world as a Roman citizen and the religious world as a Jew for a long time before he met Jesus. He was the perfect person to steward the mystery and function of the church to the generation of saints in this Church Age because he could speak to Jew and Gentile alike.

MEMBERS ALL

Paul's letters give believers a deep understanding of who they are in Christ both individually and corporately, and he makes it clear that one does not function without the other. The individual gifts will not bring forth what God wants apart from their corporate family.

Now you [collectively] are Christ's body and [individually] you are members of it, each part severally and distinct [each with his own place and function].
1 Corinthians 12:27 AMP

> **There is no verse of Scripture that says you are, yourself, the body of Christ.**

Individual gifts are best understood through corporate identity because the gifts are given to the church. There is no verse of Scripture that says you are, yourself, the body of Christ. Nowhere! The *New King James Version* says, "Now you are the body of Christ, and members individually." All of this language is collective. Even as a unique, precious individual, you are at the same time a member of Christ's body.

For as we have many members in one body, but all the members do not have the same function, so we, *being* many, are one body in Christ, and individually members of one another.

Romans 12:4-5

Individually you are a member of the body. Collectively we are the body of Christ. We are members of one another. The Holy Spirit chose the word "member" instead of "employee" or "part" because we are like a corporeal body not a corporate organization or a machine. The word "member" actually refers to a physical part of a person's body, such as a hand, foot, ear, or eye. Do you see how important your place in the local church is? Just imagine trying to function without a part of your body.

But now God has set the members, each one of them, in the body just as He pleased. And if they *were* all one member, where *would* the body *be*?

But now indeed *there are* many members, yet one body. And the eye cannot say to the hand, "I have no need of you"; nor again the head to the feet, "I have no need of you." No, much rather, those members of the body which seem to be weaker are necessary. And those *members* of the body which we think to be less honorable, on these we bestow greater honor; and our unpresentable *parts* have greater modesty, but our presentable *parts* have no need.

But God composed the body, having given greater honor to that *part* which lacks it, that there should be no schism in the body, but *that* the members should have the same care for one another. And if one member suffers, all the members suffer with *it;* or if one member is honored, all the members rejoice with *it.*

1 Corinthians 12:18-26

The body of Christ is just like a physical body. God designed our physical bodies and He has designed the spiritual body of Christ. Like the physical body, when all the members are in good health and doing what they are supposed to be doing, we feel great, we accomplish what we need to accomplish, and we enjoy life. But if our foot gets cut off, our eyes are attacked by some disease, or our heart just decides not to beat for awhile, life is not going to be all God promised it could be. That's why we have to care for one another like we are caring for ourselves—because we are caring for ourselves! When one of us gets under something we all get under it with them and move them back to being on top again. When

> Your local church is where you function in the reality of being in the universal church. The local body is where you play your part and fulfill your call as a member of Christ's body.

one of us climbs that mountain of victory, we all climb up there together and shout as one.

Being a member of the universal church is a spiritual reality, but understanding that spiritual reality is dependent upon a natural function. How do you express the spiritual reality of being in Christ? How do you as a member of His universal body become a functioning member, physically and tangibly expressing the gifts and calling God has given you? In your local body! Your local church is where you function in the reality of being in the universal church. The local body is where you play your part and fulfill your call as a member of Christ's body.

GOD'S FAMILY

When I was a child, my mother was a Christian but my father was not. He did not accept Jesus until later in life. Therefore, in my early years I really had no example of healthy, godly relationships in my home. However, my mother did something that saved my life. She took me to church every time the doors were open, and in the church I saw and was taught what the Word had to say about my being a member of God's family and how God's family members were supposed to relate to one another. I got an understanding of family and how it was to function in my local church.

Paul wrote, "For this reason I bow my knees to the Father of our Lord Jesus Christ, from whom the whole family in heaven and earth is named" (Ephesians 3:14-15)

Paul also called Jesus our joint-heir, and he made it clear that the reason we shared Jesus' inheritance was because through the new birth and the indwelling of the Holy Spirit we were God's sons and daughters with Jesus.

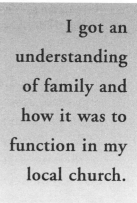

> I got an understanding of family and how it was to function in my local church.

The Spirit Himself bears witness with our spirit that we are children of God, and if children, then heirs—heirs of God and joint heirs with Christ.

Romans 8:16-17

This is legal language. The Holy Spirit is saying, "Look, you are family. You are children of God the Father and brothers and sisters with Jesus the Son, and I am living in you to reveal the full reality of all your privileges as a legal member of God's family." Hallelujah!

For whom He foreknew, He also predestined *to be* conformed to the image of His Son, that He might be the firstborn among many brethren.

Romans 8:29

God's whole plan was to have a family. He had lost the first Adam to sin, and when he lost Adam he lost all of Adam's descendants.

> God's whole plan was to have a family.

So He decided to bring forth a new family through a second Adam, Jesus, His only begotten Son. Jesus was the first to be born into this new family—a family He would never lose!

> **For I am persuaded that neither death nor life, nor angels nor principalities nor powers, nor things present nor things to come, nor height nor depth, nor any other created thing, shall be able to separate us from the love of God which is in Christ Jesus our Lord.**
>
> **Romans 8:38-39**

This also means that once we are children of our Father in Heaven, nothing can separate us from His love. Unlike our natural parents, who might not have even wanted us, who might have treated us badly, and who might want nothing to do with us, God our Father always loves us and desires to bless us. He is always there for us no matter what we've said or done to try to mess up our relationship with Him or His other children. He is involved in our lives even more than our natural fathers were.

> **Furthermore, we had earthly fathers to discipline us, and we respected them; shall we not much rather be subject to the Father of spirits, and live?**
>
> **For they disciplined us for a short time as seemed best to them, but He disciplines us for our good, so that we may share His holiness.**
>
> **Hebrews 12:9-10**

You say, "Well, I never had a father," or "My father never took any interest in me." Well, now you have a Father who is not only present but also is so interested in you that He knows how many hairs you have on your head (Luke 12:7)! Your Heavenly Father wants to help you to be all He created you to be, to be successful and happy and fulfilled. He is not standing off in the distance just watching you live your life, not caring whether you make it or not. No, by His Spirit inside your spirit He's right in the middle of everything you are thinking, saying, and doing.

There is also no sibling rivalry in God's family. Jesus is not going to get irritated with you one day and take off with your inheritance. He promised He will never leave you nor forsake you, and He will stick closer to you than any natural brother or sister ever could or would (Hebrews 13:5).

There is also no sibling rivalry in God's family.

We also have spiritual mothers and fathers in the family of God. Paul was a spiritual father. He may not have had natural children, but he had a lot of spiritual children.

> **For though you might have ten thousand instructors in Christ, yet *you do* not *have* many fathers; for in Christ Jesus I have begotten you through the gospel.**
>
> **1 Corinthians 4:15**

Maybe you never had a father or mother who enjoyed the things you enjoy or wanted to be a part of what interested you. Just ask the Holy Spirit to connect you with a spiritual father or mother who will! Or maybe you do not have natural children. When you are in the church this is not something that has to depress you or stop you from living a full life because the church is a family, God's

family. There are plenty of sons and daughters who need mothers and fathers in the faith.

Were you an only child? Did you always want brothers and sisters? Or maybe you had all brothers and wanted a sister, or had all sisters and wanted a brother. The church has what you have always wanted! Like Paul and Barnabas you are going to have such a great time with your spiritual brothers and sisters that you will travel across the country to spend time with them.

> **Then after some days Paul said to Barnabas, "Let us now go back and visit our brethren in every city where we have preached the word of the Lord, *and see* how they are doing."**
>
> Acts 15:36

The work of God in you is greater than the hurts of this life, and you will find the family you need in your local church.

I don't know what has happened in your natural family that has hurt you and held you back, but I'm telling you right now, the work of God in you is greater than the hurts of this life, and you will find the family you need in your local church. Paul knew this first-hand, and his revelation of the mystery of the church included both how we are members of Christ's body and also God's family.

You are a beloved member of God's family, with a Father who loves you so much that He sent His only begotten Son, Jesus, to die for you and give you the Holy Spirit to be with you always. This also makes you a member of the Body of

Christ the moment you are born again. In other words, you are not alone!

What Peter received and Paul revealed is what you must understand and live in today: The only way you are going to live in the reality of every blessing and great work God has for you is to take your place in your local church.

4

YOU CAN'T BE SENT OUT IF YOU AREN'T IN

You are automatically in the universal church the moment you are born again, but you have to *choose* to be committed to a local church.

You are automatically in the universal church the moment you are born again, but you have to *choose* to be committed to a local church. Being "in" for a believer in the local church means being in all the way, fully dedicating your life to do your part and encourage your brothers and sisters and all the leaders. Only then will you fully understand who you are and the part you are to play in the universal church.

God has called you out of the world to be a part of His body. That is a spiritual reality. But that spiritual reality manifests into the natural realm through the local church, where you will be discipled and grow up into the image of Christ Jesus by forming relationships and developing your gifts and calling. The local church is the key to your life in Jesus Christ. That's why I always say that if you aren't in your place you can't do your part.

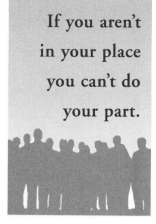

If you aren't in your place you can't do your part.

If Peter hadn't been in the Upper Room on the Day of Pentecost, he would not have been baptized in the Holy Spirit or given the first Gospel message from a born-again, Spirit-filled member of the church. He was there, so he got what God was giving out. If you are not sitting in the local church God has called you to, the anointing will come and you will not be there to receive it.

Not only are you "taught" in a local church, many things are also "caught." As you minister, grow, and learn with your brothers and sisters, your outward actions begin to change and your faith grows as your mind is renewed by the Word of God. You learn everything from how to lead someone to the Lord and pray for the sick to how a good local church is administrated. This is how all the great people of God have become great.

Not only are you "taught" in a local church, many things are also "caught."

We have already talked about Barnabas, and we saw how he encouraged the local church at Jerusalem. The leadership there sent him out to see what God was doing in

Antioch. Because he was in the church in Jerusalem, Barnabas could be sent out to Antioch, to establish the church that became one of the key missionary evangelic centers for the whole world in that time. If he hadn't been in the church at Jerusalem, he would have missed his calling. Even the Apostle Paul was sent out from the local church.

> Now in the church that was at Antioch there were certain prophets and teachers: Barnabas, Simeon who was called Niger, Lucius of Cyrene, Manaen who had been brought up with Herod the tetrarch, and Saul. As they ministered to the Lord and fasted, the Holy Spirit said, "Now separate to Me Barnabas and Saul for the work to which I have called them." Then, having fasted and prayed, and laid hands on them, they sent *them* away.
>
> Acts 13:1-3

Every person who was successful in the plan of God in the New Testament was sent out from a local church and remained connected to a local church.

The call of God was already on Saul and Barnabas, but they were actually separated and commissioned by the Holy Spirit through the elders of the local church at Antioch. Every believer in the book of Acts understood this principle. Each of them knew they had a vital role and position to fulfill in their local assembly, and as they did their part the Holy Spirit would develop their gifts and character so that He could commission them into their calling. Every person who was successful in the plan of God in the New Testament was sent out from a local church and remained connected to a local church.

TITUS WAS SENT OUT

Although Titus is not mentioned in the book of Acts, we can piece together his history from the books of Galatians, 2 Corinthians, Titus, and 2 Timothy. In chronological order, we would begin with Galatians. Paul writes,

> **Then after fourteen years I went up again to Jerusalem with Barnabas, and also took Titus with *me*. Yet not even Titus who *was* with me, being a Greek, was compelled to be circumcised.**
>
> **Galatians 2:1,3**

Barnabas, Paul, and Titus were at the church at Antioch. It had been fourteen years since Barnabas had first introduced Saul of Tarsus as a new believer to the leaders of the church at Jerusalem. By the time of these verses in Galatians, both had become leaders in the church at Antioch, and Titus was one of the men they were teaching and training there.

These verses also reveal something significant about the functioning of the local churches. They looked to the church at Jerusalem for oversight. Even the churches and their leadership were not Lone Rangers. Paul and Barnabas had been sent out by the elders of Jerusalem and were still accountable to them. This was demonstrated when disputes arose between Paul and Barnabas, and a group of believers called Judaizers. This group of

born-again Jews taught that Gentile converts should keep the Old Testament Law or they could not remain saved. Paul and Barnabas took the matter to the leaders at Jerusalem—and they took Titus as their evidence.

Titus was a Gentile, and Paul used him in Jerusalem as an example of a Gentile believer who has been circumcised of the heart and did not need to be circumcised of the flesh to prove he was a born-again child of God (Romans 2:29). This mention of Titus reveals that he was already a strong man of God, he was closely associated with Paul and Barnabas, and he was fully submitted to and involved in the local church at Antioch.

The next time we hear of Titus is many years later, when Paul stops in Troas on his way to Macedonia.

> **Furthermore, when I came to Troas to *preach* Christ's gospel, and a door was opened to me by the Lord, I had no rest in my spirit, because I did not find Titus my brother; but taking my leave of them, I departed for Macedonia.**
>
> **2 Corinthians 2:12-13**

Paul was very disappointed that he did not find Titus in Troas, but he soon met up with him in Macedonia.

> This mention of Titus reveals that he was already a strong man of God, he was closely associated with Paul and Barnabas, and he was fully submitted to and involved in the local church at Antioch.

For indeed, when we came to Macedonia, our bodies had no rest, but we were troubled on every side. Outside *were* conflicts, inside *were* fears. Nevertheless God, who comforts the downcast, comforted us by the coming of Titus, and not only by his coming, but also by the consolation with which he was comforted in you, when he told us of your earnest desire, your mourning, your zeal for me, so that I rejoiced even more.

Therefore we have been comforted in your comfort. And we rejoiced exceedingly more for the joy of Titus, because his spirit has been refreshed by you all. For if in anything I have boasted to him about you, I am not ashamed. But as we spoke all things to you in truth, even so our boasting to Titus was found true. And his affections are greater for you as he remembers the obedience of you all, how with fear and trembling you received him. Therefore I rejoice that I have confidence in you in everything.

2 Corinthians 7:5-7, 13-16

If you read through the book of 1 Corinthians, you will see that Paul had to set a lot of things in order there. They were a tremendously charismatic church, but they needed discipline and grounding in the Word of God. There were things taking place at the church that were immoral, foolish, and chaotic. After Paul's first time there, the church at Antioch had sent Titus to Corinth to help and encourage that local assembly, as well as deliver Paul's first letter to them. Isn't it interesting that the Corinthians received

Titus with fear and trembling, with as much respect for him as they had for Paul?

> So we urged Titus, that as he had begun, so he would also complete this grace in you as well.
>
> 2 Corinthians 8:6

> But thanks *be* to God who puts the same earnest care for you into the heart of Titus. For he not only accepted the exhortation, but being more diligent, he went to you of his own accord.
>
> 2 Corinthians 8:16-17

Second Corinthians tells how successful Titus' work was, but it also reveals the close relationships between Paul and Titus—a relationship that had been established at the church at Antioch.

Titus came to see Paul in Macedonia and gave Paul a great report on the church at Corinth, so Paul wrote his second letter to the Corinthians and sent Titus to deliver it. Second Corinthians tells how successful Titus' work was, but it also reveals the close relationships between Paul and Titus—a relationship that had been established at the church at Antioch.

The next time we encounter Titus is in Paul's letter to him.

> To Titus, a true son in *our* common faith:
>
> Grace, mercy, *and* peace from God the Father and the Lord Jesus Christ our Savior.

> For this reason I left you in Crete, that you should set
> in order the things that are lacking, and appoint elders in
> every city as I commanded you.
>
> Titus 1:4-5

Titus accompanied Paul to Crete, and then history tells us that he lived the rest of his life as a pastor and apostle of the churches on that island. This was no small job! The people of Crete were like a bunch of gangsters.

> For there are many rebellious people, mere talkers and
> deceivers, especially those of the circumcision group. They
> must be silenced, because they are ruining whole
> households by teaching things they ought not to teach—
> and that for the sake of dishonest gain. Even one of their
> own prophets has said, "Cretans are always liars, evil
> brutes, lazy gluttons." This testimony is true. In fact, both
> their minds and consciences are corrupted. They claim to
> know God, but by their actions they deny him. They are
> detestable, disobedient and unfit for doing anything good.
>
> Titus 1:10-13,15-16 NIV

Rebellion. Vain talking. Lying. Bad doctrine. Families falling apart. Violent tempers. Lazy gluttons. Minds and consciences corrupted. They claimed to be Christians but did not act like it. "They are detestable, disobedient, and unfit for doing anything good." These were some of the worst people to pastor! I don't know what kind of church you are in, but I think Titus probably had the worst one. Yet Paul had enough confidence in Titus to say, "See you later, Titus!" and leave him in charge. Later he sent him

a letter (the book of Titus) to tell him what to do and to encourage him in the faith.

Titus was successful in Crete, but he kept his close relationship with Paul, who was his father in the faith, until Paul's death. From 2 Timothy 4:10, it seems pretty certain that Titus visited Paul when he was imprisoned in Rome and just before he was beheaded. Overall, Paul had this to say about Titus:

> If *anyone inquires* about Titus, *he is* my partner and fellow worker concerning you. Or if our brethren *are inquired about, they are* messengers of the churches, the glory of Christ.
>
> 2 Corinthians 8:23

Titus was Paul's partner, fellow worker, and messenger of the churches. From the church at Antioch, Titus was sent out again and again. He was known by the people of that local assembly, and by the time Paul left him at Crete, he was known in many of the local churches. Titus didn't just show up somewhere and say, "Excuse me, I'd like to do something great for God here." No, the significance of his life was unveiled as he gave himself to the local body of believers and their leadership. Then the Holy Spirit could freely commission him to what he was called to do.

Titus was bold and strong and extremely productive for God because he understood that the strategic plan of God

Titus didn't just show up somewhere and say, "Excuse me, I'd like to do something great for God here."

for his time and his life were one and the same: the functioning of the local church.

TIMOTHY WAS SENT OUT

Then he came to Derbe and Lystra. And behold, a certain disciple was there, named Timothy, *the* son of a certain Jewish woman who believed, but his father *was* Greek. He was well spoken of by the brethren who were at Lystra and Iconium. Paul wanted to have him go on with him. And he took *him* and circumcised him because of the Jews who were in that region, for they all knew that his father was Greek. And as they went through the cities, they delivered to them the decrees to keep, which were determined by the apostles and elders at Jerusalem. So the churches were strengthened in the faith, and increased in number daily.

Acts 16:1-5

Paul met Timothy at the local church in Lystra, where Timothy was highly esteemed by the brethren there. Timothy was different from Titus, and we can see how Paul treated him differently. Titus was a Gentile, but Timothy was half-Jewish because his mother was Jewish. (In Judaism you are only considered a true Jew if your mother is Jewish.)

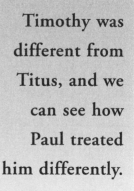

Timothy was different from Titus, and we can see how Paul treated him differently.

To Timothy, a beloved son:

Grace, mercy, *and* peace from God the Father and Christ Jesus our Lord.

I thank God, whom I serve with a pure conscience, as *my* forefathers *did,* as without ceasing I remember you in my prayers night and day, greatly desiring to see you, being mindful of your tears, that I may be filled with joy, when I call to remembrance the genuine faith that is in you, which dwelt first in your grandmother Lois and your mother Eunice, and I am persuaded is in you also.

2 Timothy 1:2-5

Paul gave Timothy almost the same greeting he gave Titus in his letter to Titus. Then he thanked God for Timothy's spiritual heritage, that the faith of his mother and grandmother had been passed on to him. However, the fact that Paul circumcised Timothy indicated that his mother and grandmother did not give him a strict Jewish upbringing. Paul took Timothy as his spiritual son and felt it was important for him to be circumcised because he ministered to so many Jews as well as Gentiles.

Again, Timothy was not somebody who walked off the street one day and told Paul,

> Timothy was well known and had established himself as a faithful servant among the believers at the church at Lystra, a church Paul and Barnabas had founded and established in Acts, chapter 14.

"Hey, God wants me to go with you on your next missionary journey." No, Timothy was well known and had established himself as a faithful servant among the believers at the church at Lystra, a church Paul and Barnabas had founded and established in Acts, chapter 14. They had an ongoing relationship with this local assembly, and so they knew Timothy and his family well.

Paul's first letter to Timothy reveals a lot about how Timothy came to understand who he was in Christ through the function of the local church at Lystra. They prophesied to him, taught him sound doctrine, and imparted gifts to him.

> **This charge I commit to you, son Timothy, according to the prophecies previously made concerning you, that by them you may wage the good warfare.**
>
> **1 Timothy 1:18**

> **Do not neglect the gift that is in you, which was given to you by prophecy with the laying on of the hands of the eldership. Meditate on these things; give yourself entirely to them, that your progress may be evident to all. Take heed to yourself and to the doctrine. Continue in them, for in doing this you will save both yourself and those who hear you.**
>
> **1 Timothy 4:14-16**

It was at the local church in Lystra that Paul heard from the Holy Spirit and said to Timothy "You are to come with me."

Paul told Timothy that he was to continue in what he had learned and received from the

church at Lystra. I have to tell you, I meet some saints of God and can tell immediately that they have never been involved in a local church. They are confused about who they are, their doctrine is all mixed up, and even though God has anointed them, they have no idea how to operate in their gift. Timothy was not like that because he had submitted to the eldership and had learned to operate in his gifts in the local assembly of believers at Lystra. He was established in the faith and in sound doctrine.

It was at the local church in Lystra that Paul heard from the Holy Spirit and said to Timothy, "You are to come with me." Timothy was one of his sons in the faith. He served beside Paul as an evangelist and later became the pastor of the church in Ephesus. Paul had the same great commendation for Timothy that he had for Titus:

Individual anointing and gifting is only truly understood through corporate relationship.

But I trust in the Lord Jesus to send Timothy to you shortly, that I also may be encouraged when I know your state. For I have no one like-minded, who will sincerely care for your state. For all seek their own, not the things which are of Christ Jesus. But you know his proven character, that as a son with *his* father he served with me in the gospel.

Philippians 2:19-22

After they had served together for years, Paul refers to Timothy the way a natural father would refer to his son. When you are in the local church and sent out from the local church, you not only find yourself and your part in God's strategic plan—you also find the richest and most satisfying relationships.

Individual anointing and gifting is only truly understood through corporate relationship. You are never going to figure out what God wants to do with you unless you are properly related to His church. Like Timothy, unless you are in you cannot be sent out.

SILAS WAS SENT OUT

Then it pleased the apostles and elders, with the whole church, to send chosen men of their own company to Antioch with Paul and Barnabas, *namely,* Judas who was also named Barsabas, and Silas, leading men among the brethren.

Acts 15:22

The first time Silas showed up was in Acts 15:22, and he was considered one of the "leading men among the brethren." We don't know how long Silas had been at the church in Jerusalem, but he had obviously grown into a mature and respected man of God by this time. When trouble arose in the church at Antioch, which had been originally established by Barnabas and Paul, the leaders in the Jerusalem church sent those they knew were up to the task of straightening things

> They sent those they knew, those who had been laboring among them, who were men of experience and authority. Silas was one of those.

out. They sent those they knew, those who had been laboring among them, who were men of experience and authority. Silas was one of those.

> Now Judas and Silas, themselves being prophets also, exhorted and strengthened the brethren with many words. And after they had stayed *there* for a time, they were sent back with greetings from the brethren to the apostles.
>
> However, it seemed good to Silas to remain there. Paul and Barnabas also remained in Antioch, teaching and preaching the word of the Lord, with many others also.
>
> Acts 15:32-35

Where did Silas and Judas become recognized prophets? Where were their gifts recognized and developed? The local church is the place where the body of Christ is edified and equipped for the work of the ministry.

> And He Himself gave some *to be* apostles, some prophets, some evangelists, and some pastors and teachers, for the equipping of the saints for the work of ministry, for the edifying of the body of Christ.
>
> Ephesians 4:11-12

The real equipping of the saints happens in the local assembly.

The real equipping of the saints happens in the local assembly. However, you have to be there in order for your gifts to be developed, for your calling to be recognized, and for the character of God to be formed in you.

Silas traveled with Paul on his second missionary journey (Acts 15:40-17:10). In Acts 16:37, after he and Paul had been beaten and thrown into prison at Philippi, Paul referred to himself and Silas as Roman citizens. From what they endured and how they praised God through it all, we know Silas was tough and spiritually mature like Paul. Whereas Timothy and Titus had been Paul's sons in the Lord, Silas was his equal.

When they got to Berea, Paul went on; but Silas stayed there with Timothy. Later, he and Timothy joined Paul in Corinth, where they helped to establish the local church there. Silas is also called by his Roman name, Silvanus.

But _as_ God _is_ faithful, our word to you was not Yes and No. For the Son of God, Jesus Christ, who was preached among you by us—by me, Silvanus, and Timothy—was not Yes and No, but in Him was Yes. For all the promises of God in Him _are_ Yes, and in Him Amen, to the glory of God through us.

2 Corinthians 1:18-20

Silas was a prophet and a preacher of the Word, and tradition tells us that eventually he became the pastor and overseer at the church at Corinth. Like Paul, he was an incredible gift to the churches, and his whole life was about building the local church. All of this happened in his life because he was faithful in the local church at Jerusalem. Because he was in, they could send him out and Paul could trust him.

PHILIP WAS SENT OUT

Now in those days, when *the number of* the disciples was multiplying, there arose a complaint against the Hebrews by the Hellenists, because their widows were neglected in the daily distribution. Then the twelve summoned the multitude of the disciples and said, "It is not desirable that we should leave the word of God and serve tables. Therefore, brethren, seek out from among you seven men of *good* reputation, full of the Holy Spirit and wisdom, whom we may appoint over this business; but we will give ourselves continually to prayer and to the ministry of the word."

And the saying pleased the whole multitude. And they chose Stephen, a man full of faith and the Holy Spirit, and Philip, Prochorus, Nicanor, Timon, Parmenas, and Nicolas, a proselyte from Antioch, whom they set before the apostles; and when they had prayed, they laid hands on them.

Acts 6:1-6

The place was the church at Jerusalem, and the church had a big problem. The Jewish widows were getting more food than the Hellenist (Greek) widows, and somebody started complaining. They were upset over food distribution! The churches today are no different. We argue over the color of our carpet, and we get mad when the pastor shows any extra favor to anyone. Every church has growing pains!

The twelve apostles got together and came up with a solution. They asked the disciples of the church to "seek out from among you" seven men. They didn't say, "put an ad in the paper for seven openings in our Food Distribution Department," and they sure didn't turn to the ones who were complaining. They also didn't go down the street to get Joe, who was a Christian but didn't come to church because he could get taught from television—they didn't even know Joe.

They didn't go visit Old Bubba, who had his own church service with his family because they were the only ones who would do what he said. What Bubba didn't understand was that when you have to adapt to other believers in the local church, when you have to crucify your flesh and "submit to one another," you make the greatest advancements in developing the character and gifts of God in your life.

> When you have to crucify your flesh and "submit to one another," you make the greatest advancements in developing the character and gifts of God in your life.

There is something about being with other believers that will cause you to grow up! There is something about teaching Sunday school or singing in the choir that gets rid of selfishness and brings forth the loving heart of a servant. And there is something about praying for the sick or giving cheerfully of your finances that activates the gifts God has given you. The local church is the place

> Philip was just another believer in the assembly of Jerusalem, but he was known to be a godly man, full of the Spirit and God's wisdom.

in which gifts and calling can flourish and hearts for God and His people can expand.

The elders of the church of Jerusalem knew this. That's why they instructed the congregation to select seven men who were "of *good* reputation, full of the Holy Spirit and wisdom." These seven men would make things right for the widows and serve them with love and honor. One of the men they chose was Philip.

Philip was just another believer in the assembly of Jerusalem, but he was known to be a godly man, full of the Spirit and God's wisdom. How was he rewarded? He became a deacon, distributing the food to the widows. It seems like such an insignificant thing, but it made a tremendous difference.

Then the word of God spread, and the number of the disciples multiplied greatly in Jerusalem, and a great many of the priests were obedient to the faith.

Acts 6:7

Not only did the church grow in numbers, but some of those numbers were Jewish priests! This happened because seven men accepted the call of God that came through the people they worshipped with. They said, "We don't want to be a problem; we want to be the answer." We don't know if any of them had ever served before. That is not even the issue. The issue was that there was a need and they said, "We want to meet that need." Like Barnabas, they became an encouragement to the church.

People ask us, "How do I get promoted in the work of God? How do I get started in the ministry I'm called to do?" We tell them to volunteer in their local church. If they see a problem, become the answer to that problem. If they see a need, meet that need the best they can. As they serve God by serving His people, He will mature them and move them into their calling.

Philip had the right attitude. He knew he wasn't just serving a bunch of complaining widows their lunch. He was building the church of Jesus Christ! He was anointed by God to push back the works of darkness by showing each widow the same love and care. Philip was one of those who destroyed the plot of the enemy to divide the church at Jerusalem!

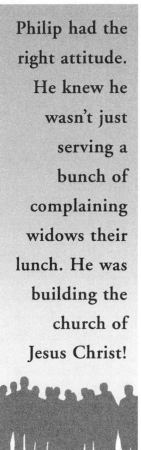

Philip had the right attitude. He knew he wasn't just serving a bunch of complaining widows their lunch. He was building the church of Jesus Christ!

In the next chapter of Acts, the devil used Saul of Tarsus to wreak havoc on the church in Jerusalem. Stephen, who was one of the seven chosen with Philip, was stoned to death. The believers were scattered, but they continued to preach Jesus to everyone they could.

Therefore those who were scattered went everywhere preaching the word. Then Philip went down to the city of Samaria and preached Christ to them. And the multitudes

with one accord heeded the things spoken by Philip, hearing and seeing the miracles which he did. For unclean spirits, crying with a loud voice, came out of many who were possessed; and many who were paralyzed and lame were healed. And there was great joy in that city.

Acts 8:4-8

Now where did Philip learn to cast out devils, heal the sick, and get people saved? How did he and the other believers have the courage to keep preaching the Word after they had just seen their beloved brother Stephen stoned to death? First, I'm sure they were inspired by how Stephen died. As the religious Jews were stoning him to death, Stephen called out, "Lord Jesus, receive my spirit…do not charge them with this sin" (Acts 7:59-60). Stephen followed Jesus' way and forgave those who were murdering him as he died. Stephen was someone who lived what he preached, and he inspired the rest of the saints to do the same.

Second, the believers in the church of Jerusalem may have had a moment of strife over the distribution of food to the widows, but they got over it! They knew nothing was going to stop the plan of God. One of their own had been stoned to death for his courage in preaching the Gospel; and although they mourned him, they kept going. Besides, they were going to see Stephen again in Heaven. He was probably up there cheering them on. They knew the family was both in Heaven and on Earth, so they picked up their armor and went on the offensive in faith.

This reminds me of the story of the missionary who had been in Africa most of his life. He came home to America in his late seventies, and he happened to be on the same ship as Theodore

Roosevelt. When they came into New York Harbor, a band was playing, balloons were flying, and the dock was filled with cheering people. He said, "Lord, there's no celebration for my homecoming."

The Lord answered him, "Son, you're not home yet."

The church at Jerusalem understood this. They knew people can quit shouting your praises here on Earth, but you'll never lose your reward in Heaven. Things might get rough down here, but everything will be glorious throughout eternity with the Lord. They knew Stephen was in a great place, and all they wanted to do was carry on his work—the work of the church.

Philip was sent out from this great church at Jerusalem. Just days before he had been serving food, but after the saints were scattered he was leading Samaria to Jesus Christ. He was holding evangelistic crusades, getting people saved and healed and set free, and establishing a new body of believers there. When the apostles in Jerusalem heard about it, they sent Peter and John to get the new converts in Samaria baptized in the Holy Ghost and to set things in order.

Philip is the only person in the New Testament referred to as an evangelist (Acts 21:8), and he stayed connected with his local church. He was never out of communication and fellowship with the church at Jerusalem. He knew that his gift could only function properly with the other gifts in the church.

> Philip is the only person in the New Testament referred to as an evangelist (Acts 21:8), and he stayed connected with his local church.

We may be the greatest preacher since Billy Graham, but if we are not serving and under the guidance and direction of a local church—as Dr. Graham has always been—that gift God put in us will never be properly developed. In fact, it might never be developed at all.

Wherever he got people saved, he needed the apostle, prophet, pastor, and teacher to come and establish a local body of believers where those new converts could become strong in the Lord. That is what happened in Samaria. After Philip evangelized the area, the others came in to establish the local church there, and Philip returned to Jerusalem to get his next assignment from the Lord.

In Acts 8:26-40, an angel appeared to Philip and told him to go south on the road from Jerusalem to Gaza. He obeyed, and he met an Ethiopian who was reading the book of Isaiah and needing instruction as to its meaning. Philip led the man to Jesus, baptized him in water, and immediately the Holy Spirit translated him to another city, where he continued to preach the Gospel. He evangelized all the way back to Jerusalem, his home church.

Remember, this is a man who began his ministry by serving lunch to the ladies of the church! Now he is one of the very few in the Bible who were translated. The life of Philip shows us something: we may be the greatest preacher since Billy Graham, but if we are not serving and under the guidance and direction of a local church—as Dr. Graham has always been—that gift God put in us will never be properly developed. In fact, it might never be developed at all.

PROMOTION AND BLESSING

On the next day we who were Paul's companions departed and came to Caesarea, and entered the house of Philip the evangelist, who was one of the seven, and stayed with him.

Acts 21:8

It has been about twenty years since Saul of Tarsus held the coats of those who stoned Stephen and consented to his death. He is now the great Apostle Paul, and Luke writes in the book of Acts that he and other companions of Paul stayed with Philip the evangelist—who is also still known as "one of the seven"! Philip is giving hospitality to the friends and companions of the very person who was responsible for the death of Stephen. He and Stephen had worked alongside one another, and were probably close. While they were serving in the local church, Saul was making plans to destroy it—but now they've come together to build it.

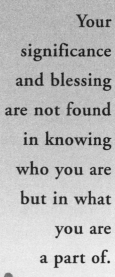

Your significance and blessing are not found in knowing who you are but in what you are a part of.

No wonder God could use Philip so mightily! He was humble. He was forgiving. And he was dedicated to building the church. He loved people, and his greatest delight was

seeing them get saved and set free from all the power of the enemy—just like the Apostle Paul. Building the church with Jesus will inspire you to overcome the most terrible obstacles and give you the courage and compassion to forgive someone who caused one of the most painful times of your life.

Acts 21:9 says Philip had four daughters who prophesied. When you give your life to the plan of God by serving His people in the local church, you touch the heart of God. There is no telling how much He will bless you. When you take care of His family, He takes care of your family. Your significance and blessing are not found in knowing who you are but in what you are a part of.

What will you become if you give yourself to the plan of God in the local church? Only God knows the extent of your call to His people and His blessings for you as you fulfill that call. I know believers all over the world who are much more talented than we are, but for some reason aren't being used by God in any meaningful way. Then you ask them, "Where do you go to church?"

Their reply is something like this, "Uh, well, you know, I was going here, but the music was just not my style, and then the pastor said something that I really didn't like, so I left. I just haven't found any church that I like." Although they have some idea of what their gifts and calling are, they have no idea how God wants to use them because they are not in!

God is operating the same way now as He did in the book of Acts. He will work in you and through you the same way He did in the lives of Titus, Timothy, Silas, and Philip. When you are firmly committed in your church, God can send you out to do mighty exploits in His name.

HOW TO WALK IN OVERCOMING FAITH AND POWER

Do you want to be like the heroes of faith in Hebrews 11? After reading what the Bible says about them, you may change your mind!

...who through faith subdued kingdoms, worked righteousness, obtained promises, stopped the mouths of lions, quenched the violence of fire, escaped the edge of the sword, out of weakness were made strong, became valiant in battle, turned to flight the armies of the aliens. Women received their dead raised to life again. Others were tortured, not accepting deliverance, that they might obtain a better resurrection. Still others had trial of mockings and scourgings, yes, and of chains and imprisonment. They were stoned, they were sawn in

two, were tempted, were slain with the sword. They wandered about in sheepskins and goatskins, being destitute, afflicted, tormented—of whom the world was not worthy.

Hebrews 11:33-38

These men and women of God fulfilled God's redemptive purposes for their times, but it cost them something. Why did they do it? The Bible tells us that too.

And all these, having obtained a good testimony through faith, did not receive the promise, God having provided something better for us, that they should not be made perfect apart from us.

Hebrews 11:39-40

> Every one of the Old Testament heroes of faith fulfilled their part in God's plan for their day for the same reason: they were looking to receive the promise of our day!

Every one of the Old Testament heroes of faith fulfilled their part in God's plan for their day for the same reason: they were looking to receive the promise of our day! They knew that playing their part in their day would one day restore them fully to God. The church was a mystery to them, but they knew something incredible was going to happen! When Abraham laid his son on the altar of sacrifice, when Moses brought God's people out of Egypt, when Noah built the ark, and when Rahab believed God and received the spics; they all did it with their eyes set on our day.

I hear people say, "I can't wait to get to Heaven and talk with Moses, to hear how he spoke to the rock and water came bursting out." But Moses would probably interrupt them and say, "Tell me what it is like to have God's Spirit come inside you and make you new, to represent Him in all His glory to the lost. You know, I just experienced His glory for a short time on the mountain. It stayed on me for a little while, but eventually it was gone. What is it like to walk around in His glory and show His glory to the world?"

We need to wake up to what God has done for us and in us; then we can wake up to what He wants to do through us! When we truly get that revelation, we will have the courage and joy to pay whatever price we need to pay to do our part in His plan for today, to do our part in the church. Like those who have gone before us, this is how we can walk in overcoming faith and power.

> We need to wake up to what God has done for us and in us; then we can wake up to what He wants to do through us!

PAUL'S LIGHT AFFLICTION

The Church Age is marked by the unprecedented release of God's grace and therefore the greatest dispensation that has ever been; but it is not an easy day. The book of Acts tells about men and women of God taking hold of the Word of God and not

letting go—and they had plenty of trouble doing that. Some of them had more trouble than you or I might ever see.

Do you want to impact your generation as Paul did?

> From the Jews five times I received forty *stripes* minus one. Three times I was beaten with rods; once I was stoned; three times I was shipwrecked; a night and a day I have been in the deep; *in* journeys often, *in* perils of waters, *in* perils of robbers, *in* perils of *my own* countrymen, *in* perils of the Gentiles, *in* perils in the city, *in* perils in the wilderness, *in* perils in the sea, *in* perils among false brethren; in weariness and toil, in sleeplessness often, in hunger and thirst, in fastings often, in cold and nakedness—besides the other things, what comes upon me daily: my deep concern for all the churches.
>
> 2 Corinthians 11:24-28

In 2 Timothy 4:16 Paul says that every person deserted him when he really needed them.

> At my first defense no one stood with me, but all forsook me. May it not be charged against them.
>
> But the Lord stood with me and strengthened me, so that the message might be preached fully through me, and *that* all the Gentiles might hear. Also I was delivered out of the mouth of the lion.
>
> 2 Timothy 4:16-17

In these passages of Scripture, what kept Paul going when he was betrayed, deserted, attacked, and tortured? In verse 17 he said that the Lord stood with him and strengthened him. Why didn't Jesus just take him to Heaven and give him all his rewards? Jesus wanted him to fulfill his calling, "That by me the preaching might be fully known, and that all the Gentiles might hear." What did the Gentiles need to hear? The Good News, which was that the grace of God had been released to them through the death and resurrection of Jesus Christ.

Every place Paul went he encountered opposition. Sometimes it was from people and sometimes it was from nature, but he always knew the devil was behind it and that God was much greater than the devil. He knew the powers of Hell could not stop the plan of God—His church. Being fully persuaded of this, in all that he suffered Paul did not magnify his difficulties. You know what he called them? He called them "light affliction"!

> **For all things *are* for your sakes, that grace, having spread through the many, may cause thanksgiving to abound to the glory of God.**
>
> **Therefore we do not lose heart. Even though our outward man is perishing, yet the inward *man* is being renewed day by day. For our light affliction, which is but for a moment, is working for us a far more exceeding *and* eternal weight of glory, while we do not look at the things which are seen, but at the things which are not seen. For the**

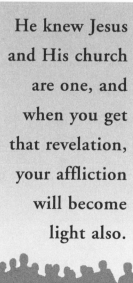

He knew Jesus and His church are one, and when you get that revelation, your affliction will become light also.

things which are seen *are* temporary, but the things which are not seen *are* eternal.

2 Corinthians 4:15-18

Why could Paul call being stoned and left for dead, thrown out of towns, rejected and mocked, beaten and put in stocks, shipwrecked, sleeplessness, hunger and thirst, constant danger, and dealing with false brethren "light affliction"? Again, he said it himself in verse 15: He did it all for the church because the church revealed the grace and glory of God. Paul was consumed with what God was doing on the Earth through the church. He knew Jesus and His church are one, and when you get that revelation, your affliction will become light also.

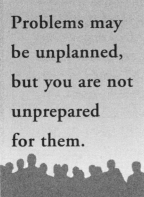

Problems may be unplanned, but you are not unprepared for them.

Problems may be unplanned, but you are not unprepared for them because of your relationship to God through Jesus Christ. You know you can persevere in faith because, like the heroes of faith, you know what's coming. You know the results of walking in faith are multitudes coming into God's kingdom and turning their families, neighborhoods, cities, and nations to Jesus Christ. You know that one day every eye will see and every ear will hear the truth that Jesus is Lord and there is no other God but our God.

When you play your part in your church, when you lay down your life for your brothers and sisters and those who will become your brothers and sisters, then you can count it all as joy when you encounter anything that opposes or tries to stop the plan of God in your life. You can shake it off and keep going because nothing and no one can stop the plan of God, which is the church, and you are playing your part in His church!

All mighty men and women of God are empowered by knowing their time and doing their part in their time. Any one of them could have said what Paul said just before he was beheaded by the Romans:

> For I am already being poured out as a drink offering, and the time of my departure is at hand. I have fought the good fight, I have finished the race, I have kept the faith. Finally, there is laid up for me the crown of righteousness, which the Lord, the righteous Judge, will give to me on that Day, and not to me only but also to all who have loved His appearing.
>
> 2 Timothy 4:6-8

> **You can shake it off and keep going because nothing and no one can stop the plan of God, which is the church, and you are playing your part in His church!**

Paul said, 'I'm looking up! My eyes are set above. I have lived every day of my life with the end in mind." He didn't end his journey crawling over the finish line. He ran his race with his eye on the prize of the high calling of God in Christ Jesus (Philippians 3:14). What was his high calling? What part did he play in God's strategic plan for his time? Paul completed the Word of God and revealed the mystery of the church, which was God's strategic plan for our time. He dispensed to us the revelation of grace

through the shed blood and resurrected life of Jesus Christ. He defined our time and our part to play in God's redemptive plan.

Paul also said, "and not to me only but also to all who have loved His appearing." That means all the saints he labored with as well as you and me. We are included in this great adventure of faith, this dispensation of the grace of God, by simply loving His appearing. What does that mean? It means we live our lives today with the end in mind. We never take our eyes off the prize— eternity with Jesus and our Father in Heaven. And when our eyes are on the prize, we just naturally want to get as many going with us as possible. We don't want anyone to miss the blessings of God in this life or the next.

COUNT IT ALL JOY

Paul could have handled things differently. He could have just talked about all the terrible things everyone did to him, all the unfair and unjust experiences of his life, and how they weren't right. Well, maybe all those things weren't right, but Paul decided to keep his heart right toward God and toward His people. He knew he could have trouble, but trouble didn't have to have him!

> He knew he could have trouble, but trouble didn't have to have him!

You have to learn how to shake off your trials and tribulations, because that's what those who have gone before you did. In Acts 13 Paul and Barnabas saw nearly the entire city of Antioch come to Jesus, but the religious Jews got jealous and stirred up those who hadn't gotten saved to kick Paul and Barnabas out of town.

And the word of the Lord was being spread throughout all the region. But the Jews stirred up the devout and prominent women and the chief men of the city, raised up persecution against Paul and Barnabas, and expelled them from their region. But they shook off the dust from their feet against them, and came to Iconium. And the disciples were filled with joy and with the Holy Spirit.

Acts 13:49-52

You know how the disciples shook off all their troubles, the rejection, and all the persecution? Verse 52 says, "And the disciples were filled with joy and with the Holy Spirit." If anyone runs you out of town for preaching the Gospel and telling the truth, just get out in front of them and act like it's a parade! Start praying in the Spirit and let the joy of the Lord be your strength (Nehemiah 8:10). Like Paul and Barnabas, you can have joy because you know what God is doing. You know how God is using you today will bring His will to pass tomorrow because His plan cannot fail.

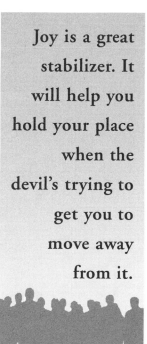

Joy is a great stabilizer. It will help you hold your place when the devil's trying to get you to move away from it.

Joy is a great stabilizer. It will help you hold your place when the devil's trying to get you to move away from it. James, the pastor

of the church at Jerusalem, said that whenever trials and tribulations come, you are to count them all joy.

My brethren, count it all joy when you fall into various trials, knowing that the testing of your faith produces patience. But let patience have *its* perfect work, that you may be perfect and complete, lacking nothing.

James 1:2-4

When you are having all kinds of trouble, you must learn to count God's way. Instead of saying, "One lie plus one lie equals a day of double lies," say, "One lie plus one lie equals a day of double joy." Pastor James told his congregation to count it ALL joy. "One disappointment yesterday plus two disappointments last week equals three times the joy because God works everything to the good of His church" (Romans 8:28)! Count it all joy.

Your unsaved friends and family won't be able to figure it out, so don't try to explain to them why you have this radiant smile on your face in the midst of a terrible trial. You'll waste your time trying to get them to see something they can't see. They are never going to count the way you count or shake off their problems and troubles by counting it all joy and being full of the Holy Ghost. However, seeing you do it will cause them to wonder what you've got that they haven't got!

Every human being has trouble. We who live in the Church Age, even with the Holy Spirit and the Word of God working in us, still go through flood and fire. I don't have to be a prophet to tell you I know you've either had trouble, you're in trouble, or you're headed for trouble! Jesus said we would all have trouble.

I have told you these things, so that in me you may have peace. In this world you will have trouble. But take heart! I have overcome the world.

John 16:33 NIV

Jesus didn't say, "Hang your head down, give up, shut up, and just quit when trouble comes. It's too much for you." He said, "Be of good cheer! I have overcome the world. I have already defeated anything that is trying to defeat you. You are My body, and this is your time! You can have peace and joy knowing that every trial and trouble is nothing more than another opportunity to reveal My love and resurrection power to everyone around you." Hallelujah!

LOVE NEVER FAILS

Our brothers and sisters in the book of Acts and all the heroes of faith in the Old Testament not only had to contend with enemies outside the church, but some of their worst troubles came from each other! However, they understood that they either would sink or swim together. Paul wrote that God "made us alive **together** with Christ (by grace you have been saved), and raised *us* up **together**, and made *us* sit **together** in the heavenly *places* in Christ Jesus" (Ephesians 2:5-6, bold mine).

We are members individually, and God sees us as Christ's body. He sees you and me in light of how we are "fitted together" in His church.

> "God made us alive together, raised us up together, and made us sit together in the heavenly places in Christ Jesus."

Now, therefore, you are no longer strangers and foreigners, but fellow citizens with the saints and members of the household of God, having been built on the foundation of the apostles and prophets, Jesus Christ Himself being the chief cornerstone, in whom the whole building, being fitted together, grows into a holy temple in the Lord, in whom you also are being built together for a dwelling place of God in the Spirit.

Ephesians 2:19-22

> Our local churches give the unbelieving world the revelation and picture of the universal church and body of Christ. The way we relate to one another reveals Jesus to the world around us.

You are not alone. You are a citizen, a member of God's household and family, an integral part of the Lord's body and the holy habitation of saints in which God now dwells. You are who you were created to be and you are able to do all you were created to do by being a part of a local assembly of His people. How do you grow in holiness and become that vessel of honor for the Lord? By being "fitted together" in your local church.

These verses in Ephesians 2 tell us how we are to function as a local body of believers, an *ekklesia* or assembly of those God has called out from the world. Our local churches give the unbelieving world the revelation and picture of the universal church and body of Christ. The way we relate to one another reveals Jesus to the world around us. That's why Jesus prayed,

"I do not pray for these alone, but also for those who will believe in Me through their word; that they all may be one, as You, Father, *are* in Me, and I in You; that they also may be one in Us, that the world may believe that You sent Me. And the glory which You gave Me I have given them, that they may be one just as We are one: I in them, and You in Me; that they may be made perfect in one, and that the world may know that You have sent Me, and have loved them as You have loved Me."

John 17:20-23

How is the world going to know God loves them and that He sent Jesus to redeem them and restore them? How will they marvel at the glory and goodness of the Lord? They will know and see when we love each other as He has loved us, when we forgive each other as He forgave us, and when we are one as He and the Father are one. That's why Paul went on to write,

I, therefore, the prisoner of the Lord, beseech you to walk worthy of the calling with which you were called, with all lowliness and gentleness, with longsuffering, bearing with one another in love, endeavoring to keep the unity of the Spirit in the bond of peace.

Ephesians 4:1-3

In our ministry there are three of us on the road together, and we also have some people working in the office at home. Each one of us has things in our lives that the others have to overlook, and

the only way to do that is to pray and walk in God's love. There are biblical principles to deal with someone if they are in sin or having a severe problem, but every one of these begins with love.

FORGIVENESS

We have come to the most significant time in human history because we live in the light of God's redemption and the authority of the name of Jesus. He freed us from the power of sin and has stripped the devil and all his demons of any authority or hold they had on us. That's why the church began at a place of victory. We don't have to get the victory because Jesus already got it!

Jesus told us how we are to operate in the victory He obtained for us. He told us it wasn't all about power; it was also about character— His character. He said that His power wouldn't properly work *for us* if His character wasn't working *in us*.

> **He said that His power wouldn't properly work *for us* if His character wasn't working *in us*.**

So Jesus answered and said to them, "Have faith in God. For assuredly, I say to you, whoever says to this mountain, 'Be removed and be cast into the sea,' and does not doubt in his heart, but believes that those things he says will be done, he will have whatever he says. Therefore I say to you, whatever things you ask when you pray, believe that you receive *them,* and you will have *them.*

"And whenever you stand praying, if you have anything against anyone, forgive him, that your Father in heaven may also forgive you your trespasses. But if you do not forgive, neither will your Father in heaven forgive your trespasses."

Mark 11:22-26

Jesus said we have such authority in His name and as His body that whatever we say—as long as we believe it in our hearts and have faith God will do it—then we can have whatever we say. Now that's power! But there's a catch. He also said that if we didn't love and forgive as He loved and forgave us, then we could forget about getting our prayers answered. The Apostle Paul wrote later in Galatians 5:6 that our faith in God and His Word, which is the key to everything in the Christian life, works by love. If we don't have love, our faith will fade and our prayers will be weak and ineffective.

The greatest act of love happened on the Cross, when Jesus said, "Father, forgive them, for they do not know what they do" (Luke 23:34). He forgave us when we were the ones who put Him on the Cross. While we were making Him suffer and die, He forgave us. In the same way, when we encounter people in and out of the church who make us suffer or even want to kill us, we are to forgive them.

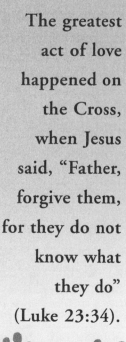

The greatest act of love happened on the Cross, when Jesus said, "Father, forgive them, for they do not know what they do" (Luke 23:34).

If we forgive in the midst of our suffering like Jesus did, we will walk in His resurrection power.

To walk out the strategic plan of God by doing your part in your local church, you are going to have to walk in forgiveness. When the pastor doesn't do what you think he should do, you are going to have to let it go and trust God. When Sister So-and-So snubs you and doesn't invite you to her party, you have to forgive her and put her in God's hands. As long as God has called you to be a part of that assembly of believers, you need to forgive and let it go.

All of us are more often tempted to quit when we are angry, hurt, or feeling sorry for ourselves. Whenever we do this we are strengthening our flesh, which makes it very hard for us to yield to the Holy Spirit and receive God's Word. Everything we hear, read, and are taught from that moment on is filtered through our selfish refusal to forgive and be reconciled.

What moves you controls you.

At times like these you need to remember: Whatever moves you controls you.

On the other hand, if we would just hold our tongue when we want to tell somebody off, put our hands to the plow, forgive, and refuse to take up an offense— then we are going to make great progress. By doing that in the place God has called us to, we also help the whole church to progress. We see the big picture: It's not just about us; it's about the plan of God working through us as a church.

Physical bodies have malfunctions and natural families have dysfunctions, and so you might as well accept the fact that the only perfect body and family are in Heaven! Until I get to Heaven or Jesus comes back and puts me in my resurrection body, I am going to have to deal with the devil, the world, and my flesh. That means I am going to have to deal with these issues in my local church.

Only by choosing to get along, to love, and to forgive my church family will I become like Jesus. If I'm not connecting with my brothers and sisters, I will remain a spiritual baby, will be no good to anyone, and will not be effective in what God has called me to do.

I also have to realize that the devil will always poke at that soft place where I have been hurt. He'll make sure that Sister So-and-So is the first person I see when I walk into the sanctuary, so I'll have to put a smile on my face and force myself to say, "Hi! My, you look great. What have you been doing?" But choosing to forgive and go on as though nothing happened is one step closer to my being completely healed of that old hurt and fully functioning in the capacity God has called me to function.

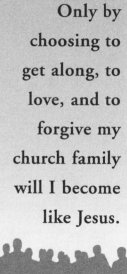

Only by choosing to get along, to love, and to forgive my church family will I become like Jesus.

I would never experience this kind of growth just sitting in my recliner, watching Christian TV, and thinking I'm such a vital part of the universal church. I might be learning some things, but until I put them into practice serving in my local church, what I am learning is not real. I am living in a dream world—and the devil has deceived me into complete uselessness!

Being active and participating in your local church is going to place you in a position where you will have every opportunity to develop the character of God and all the fruit of the Spirit. You will get the chance to refuse to harbor resentment and bitterness of any kind. Many doors will open to you that will tempt you to think and say things that will hurt and hinder your brothers and sisters. Instead, you will grow in the character of Christ by thinking and saying, "I forgive. I am a forgiver. I've been forgiven. Freely I've received, and freely I give."

> When believers are in one accord, getting along and loving and forgiving one another, supernatural things happen.

When you understand God's plan for your time, it helps you not to take offense or to hold a grudge. Your faith will be strong because you are a lover and a forgiver of the saints. Your heart will be right with God and with your brothers and sisters, and that translates into all the resurrection power of Jesus Christ flowing through your life: You can have whatever you believe in your heart and say with your mouth.

CORPORATE ANOINTING

When believers are in one accord, getting along and loving and forgiving one another, supernatural things happen. They were in one accord in the Upper Room on the Day of Pentecost and the Holy Ghost fell on them. They spoke in tongues, Peter preached the first "Holy Ghost and Fire" Gospel message, and three thousand people received Jesus as the Messiah. The corporate anointing of 150 believers did that!

Not long after that, persecution and suffering began in the church. Stephen and others were martyred for their faith, and many others were put in prison and separated from their families. But the saints stuck together, and God continued to do miracles in their midst.

> **Now about that time Herod the king stretched out *his* hand to harass some from the church. Then he killed James the brother of John with the sword. And because he saw that it pleased the Jews, he proceeded further to seize Peter also. Now it was *during* the Days of Unleavened Bread. So when he had arrested him, he put *him* in prison, and delivered *him* to four squads of soldiers to keep him, intending to bring him before the people after Passover.**

> **Acts 12:1-4**

When the Jewish leaders who opposed the Gospel killed John's brother James and threw Peter in jail, the saints had plenty of reason to be discouraged and afraid. They chose not to be! They chose to pray instead.

> **Peter was therefore kept in prison, but constant prayer was offered to God for him by the church. Now behold, an angel of the Lord stood by *him,* and a light shone in the prison; and he struck Peter on the side and raised him up, saying, "Arise quickly!" And his chains fell off *his* hands. Then the angel said to him, "Gird**

yourself and tie on your sandals"; and so he did. And he said to him, "Put on your garment and follow me." So he went out and followed him, and did not know that what was done by the angel was real, but thought he was seeing a vision.

Acts 12:5,7-9

> Nothing reveals Jesus to a lost and dying sinner like the corporate anointing of God working through His church.

Nothing reveals Jesus to a lost and dying sinner like the corporate anointing of God working through His church. Amazing and astounding things—impossible things—happen when we agree not to let go until the devil is defeated and God's will has been accomplished in someone's life. Peter was so stunned by what happened to him that he thought he was having a vision! He wasn't the only one who didn't understand what had happened at first.

And as Peter knocked at the door of the gate, a girl named Rhoda came to answer. When she recognized Peter's voice, because of *her* gladness she did not open the gate, but ran in and announced that Peter stood before the gate. But they said to her, "You are beside yourself!" Yet she kept insisting that it was so. So they said, "It is his angel."

Now Peter continued knocking; and when they opened *the door* and saw him, they were astonished.

Acts 12:13-16

Astonishing things happen when we gather together to pray. You can pray in faith in your prayer closet and get great results, but there is something even more powerful about praying and agreeing with your brothers and sisters. The Old Testament gives us an explanation of this. Deuteronomy 32:30 talks about one putting a thousand to flight and two putting ten thousand to flight. In God's kingdom, the power of God or anointing on our prayers is multiplied by ten with every person who prays.

This multiplied anointing and power applies to everything in the Christian life. When we are together on Sunday morning, it's a lot easier to get people saved, healed, and delivered because the corporate anointing of God is really tangible. We are greater together than we are alone!

We are greater together than we are alone!

I know there are times when it is just Jesus and I facing the enemy. Like Daniel, I stand on God's Word, follow His Spirit, and my faith in Him and what He's doing in me and through me in His church. Then He carries me right out of that lion's den and into the victory zone. But most of the time I am not alone, and He planned it that way. He put me in a body, a family, and an assembly of believers where I can get everything He wants to give me and at the same time give everything He has put in me to others.

If you want to realize your full potential in your time and truly walk in the miraculous power, godly character, and courage of the saints in the book of Acts, your first move must be to get plugged in to your local church. It is this simple key that will set you on the path to walking in overcoming faith and power.

YOUR IDENTITY
IS IN HIM

People have always tried to define their generation with a name. Some of the names they have taken are the Hippies, the Baby Boomers, Generation X, the Millennium Generation, and even the Lost Generation! These names are supposed to sum up the value and significance of their lives, give them a cool identity, and make them feel like they are a part of something important.

Two of the most important needs a person is born with are: to be loved and valued, and to be a part of a family or group that establishes and reinforces their identity. Only through Jesus Christ can God meet these needs in our lives. When we are born again, we discover that our Father has met both of those needs by giving our generation an identity. We are the Church.

The number one term that identifies a Christian in the New Testament is "in Christ" or "in Christ Jesus." Here are just a few of the many verses of Scripture that refer to you in this way.

Therefore, if anyone *is* in Christ, *he is* a new creation; old things have passed away; behold, all things have become new.

2 Corinthians 5:17

There is therefore now no condemnation to those who are in Christ Jesus.

Romans 8:1

Now He who establishes us with you in Christ and has anointed us *is* God.

2 Corinthians 1:21

There is neither Jew nor Greek, there is neither slave nor free, there is neither male nor female; for you are all one in Christ Jesus.

Galatians 3:28

To the church of God which is at Corinth, to those who are sanctified in Christ Jesus.

1 Corinthians 1:2

Yes, and all who desire to live godly in Christ Jesus will suffer persecution.

2 Timothy 3:12

Those who revile your good conduct in Christ may be ashamed.

1 Peter 3:16

But of Him you are in Christ Jesus, who became for us wisdom from God—and righteousness and sanctification

and redemption—that, as it is written, *"He who glories, let him glory in the LORD."*

1 Corinthians 1:30-31

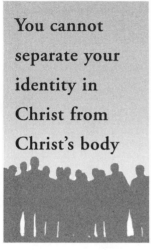

You cannot separate your identity in Christ from Christ's body

You say, "What is it about understanding who I am in Christ that's so important?" Understanding who you are in Christ is important because that is your identity! Apart from Him you are nothing. You have no purpose. You have no gifts. You have no calling. You are going nowhere fast, and you are probably walking in fear and confusion as you go. The key to unlocking your identity in Christ, however, is totally dependent upon your involvement in the local church. You cannot separate your identity in Christ from Christ's body. You are in Christ's body, the church. That is how you are identified in your time: Generation In Christ.

Without participating in the local assembly of saints, your revelation of who you are in Christ is shallow at best, next to nothing at worst. That is because you are made for the church. It's not all about you; it's about Him expressing Himself through His body, taking care of His body, and glorifying His body. If you want to discover your true identity, you must participate in His body. That is why God instituted the local assembly as His witness to the world.

GETTING TO KNOW YOU

Kenneth E. Hagin, a great Bible teacher and father in the faith, used to say that if you didn't like yourself or you were not happy with the way your life was, then you should pray the prayer in Ephesians 1:17-23 every day for six months. At the end of that time, your life would be different. He knew this was a prayer that released the revelation of who Christ Jesus is and who you are in Him.

Paul introduced this prayer in Ephesians in the verses just before it.

Therefore I also, after I heard of your faith in the Lord Jesus and your love for all the saints, do not cease to give thanks for you, making mention of you in my prayers.

Ephesians 1:15-16

This raises an important point. We pray so fervently for our unsaved loved ones and friends to be saved, but Paul said that he prayed for these Ephesians *after* he heard of their faith in Jesus. We need to be praying for one another as much as we pray for those who are lost; and if Paul prayed this prayer for those saints, we need to be praying this prayer for ourselves as well.

...that the God of our Lord Jesus Christ, the Father of glory, may give to you the spirit of wisdom and revelation in the knowledge of Him, the eyes of your understanding being enlightened; that you may know what is the hope of His calling, what are the riches of the glory of His inheritance in the saints, and what *is* the exceeding greatness of His power toward us who believe, according to the working of His mighty power which He worked in Christ when He raised Him from the dead and seated *Him* at His right hand in the heavenly *places,* far above all principality and power and might and

dominion, and every name that is named, not only in this age but also in that which is to come. And He put all *things* under His feet, and gave Him *to be* head over all *things* to the church, which is His body, the fullness of Him who fills all in all.

Ephesians 1:17-23

If you pray this over yourself, you are asking God to give you a spirit of wisdom and revelation in the knowledge of Christ, so that you will fully understand who Christ is and all He has done for you. You are praying for the eyes of your understanding to be enlightened or to be opened and to see clearly, so that you can know and understand the hope of His calling.

THE HOPE OF HIS CALLING

Notice that it is *His* calling. It is not your calling. Your calling is embedded in His calling.

...that you may know what is the hope of His calling.

Ephesians 1:18

Notice that it is *His* calling. It is not your calling. Your calling is embedded in His calling. If you don't understand that it is *His* calling—not yours—then you will believe it came from you and is all about you. Your calling does not originate with you; it originates with Him. When you get hooked up with His calling, He can reveal yours.

Romans 11:29 talks about the gifts (plural) and calling (singular) of God. The gifts are given to fulfill the call. This understanding of His calling is important because it is foundational to your identity in Him. If you think your calling is founded on what you've done, your dreams, your abilities, and your talents, then you will have cracks in your foundation because it is based on you. When those cracks begin to shift your life, you are going to want to move! But when your foundation is His calling, you are on a firm foundation. There is no possibility of cracks because your calling is based on who He is and what He has done not who you are and what you have done.

I love this paraphrase of Ephesians 1:17 from *The Distilled Bible* that says, "I pray that you new Christians will understand the mighty position with Christ which your congregations occupy." The hope of His calling is the mighty position you occupy in your local church in Christ. His calling is your hope! If you are without hope, it might be because you have not taken your place in the congregation He is calling you to.

Ephesians 1:17 answers the questions: Why are you here? Who determines what your generation is called? What is the significance of your life? The answer is found when you see what Christ has done and the power that is at work in His church. When you understand what He's doing, it will change what you're doing. It will give you a lasting hope because you will know His calling is your calling.

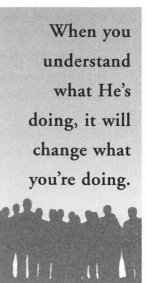

When you understand what He's doing, it will change what you're doing.

Your identity is wrapped up in Him and the hope of His calling.

THE GLORY OF HIS INHERITANCE

...what are the riches of the glory of His inheritance in the saints.

Ephesians 1:18

If your calling is His calling, His inheritance is your inheritance. You are a joint-heir with Jesus (Romans 8:17). That's good news! You not only share in His calling; you also share in everything He has inherited as the Lord of Glory. In fact, one Greek scholar states that the Greek language takes this a step further. He says,

> The words "in the saints" are locative of sphere. God's inheritance is within the sphere of the saints. That is, the phrase "in the sphere of the saints" is definitive of the word "inheritance." This takes us back to verse 11 where Paul says we saints were made God's inheritance. In verse 18, Paul prays that we might know how precious the saints are in God's eyes as His inheritance. He is glorified in His saints, and this glory is valuable. It is part of the wealth that God possesses, dearer to Him than all the splendors of creation.[1]

> **He bled and died and rose again because He was restoring His Father's inheritance: us!**

Later, Paul is going to write in Ephesians 5:25 that Jesus gave Himself for the church.

124

He bled and died and rose again because He was restoring His Father's inheritance: us! Jesus did everything for His church. Paul wrote in Titus 2:14, "Who gave himself for us, that he might redeem us from all iniquity, and purify unto himself a peculiar people, zealous of good works." (KJV)

Your identity is the glory of His inheritance because you *are* the glory of His inheritance!

HIS GREAT POWER TOWARD US

...and what *is* the exceeding greatness of His power toward us who believe.

Ephesians 1:19

Paul didn't just add these words because He needed to stretch out the page. He was trying to find words strong enough to express what the Holy Spirit was showing him. Furthermore, he was talking about you and me because the exceeding greatness of His power is toward *us* who believe. His power is toward *us!* The Holy Spirit is giving Paul a corporate view. Together we reveal His heart and mind to the world around us.

> His power is toward *us!* The Holy Spirit is giving Paul a corporate view.

The exceeding greatness of His power is toward you but it is bigger than you. His power is effectual and accomplishes the will of God through you as a member of His body. And what is His will? What is all His power for? Our local churches are to be beacons of light in a dark world. Just the sight of a cross on our

church buildings reminds the people in our communities that Jesus lived and died and rose from the dead, and He has a people who can show them the way to know Him.

I'll never forget the story about when Dwight D. Eisenhower, as Commander of the Allied Forces during World War II, went into Germany and found the Nazi death camps. He made all the people who lived in the area view the evidence of the atrocities that had occurred there. He made them take pictures, and he had people record what they saw. He made them bury the dead.

When asked why he did this, General Eisenhower answered that he knew the day would come when somebody would say that this never happened, and he wanted an overwhelming amount of physical evidence and eye-witness testimonies to prove that it did happen. He wanted to make sure that generations to follow would never doubt it or forget it.

When I heard that story, I thought about the last words Jesus spoke to his disciples. He said,

> **"But you shall receive power when the Holy Spirit has come upon you; and you shall be witnesses to Me in Jerusalem, and in all Judea and Samaria, and to the end of the earth."**

Acts 1:8

The power is toward us to do the will of the Father: to be witnesses of who Jesus is, what He has done, and what He is doing right now: building His church. The devil just hates it when God's redeemed people get together and get bold! Boldness and unity attract miracles, but they also attract persecution. If we can move through the persecution in faith and continue to let Jesus use us to build His church, we are going to see more miraculous things happen. The devil cannot stop us!

You have a part to play in the plan of God, which is part of your identity and significance, but what God is doing is bigger than your part. Your part has no meaning or purpose apart from the part that the other members of the body play. That's why this is not just power. This is "the exceeding greatness of His power" because it is being worked through all of us, not just one of us. How exceedingly great is His power?

This is "the exceeding greatness of His power" because it is being worked through all of us, not just one of us.

> ...which He worked in Christ when He raised Him from the dead and seated *Him* at His right hand in the heavenly *places*.

> Ephesians 1:20

There are those two words again: "in Christ." The exceeding greatness of His power was worked in Christ when He raised Jesus from the dead and seated Him at His right hand in Heaven. The greatest power God ever demonstrated was when He raised Jesus from the dead, and that same power is working in you right now!

Your identity is founded on the greatest power ever demonstrated in the history of mankind.

YOU SHARE HIS ETERNAL POSITION

...far above all principality and power and might and dominion, and every name that is named, not only in this age but also in that which is to come.

Ephesians 1:21

Stop and dwell for a moment on the two words "far above." The Apostle Paul was not describing a position that was just a little bit above, nor was he recounting some nail-biting, overtime victory. This wasn't winning by a nose or just barely beating out the competition. This was FAR ABOVE absolutely anyone and anything that has any authority or power in Heaven or on Earth *or has ever had or will ever have* any authority or power in Heaven or on Earth. This is a once-and-for-all-time, runaway victory! There is nothing anywhere in any time that has been done or "worked" that is greater than what God did in Christ. Nothing even comes close.

> There is nothing that has ever been done that is greater than what God did in Jesus Christ. Nothing even comes close.

God raised Jesus up and set Him above *all* principalities, powers, might, dominion, and anything or anybody that has a name not only in the time in which He raised Him but also in all time to come. In my dictionary, and I think this is true for your dictionary too, "all" means all. There are no exceptions. Jesus Christ has been seated above *all* for *all time*.

Jesus said in Matthew 16:18 that the gates of Hades would not prevail against the church. The truth here is parallel to Ephesians 1:17-23, but it is different because of timing. In Matthew Jesus gave a preview of what would be the result of His death and resurrection. He knew it was coming, but they didn't. However, in Ephesians Paul prayed for the church to see that they were the result of what Jesus had already done.

Jesus didn't come to Earth to get authority over the enemy; He came to obtain it *for us*. "And the gates of Hell shall not prevail against the church" was the promise to Peter, but Paul lived the reality of it and so do we. We are now seated with Him, far above all principality, power, might, dominion, and every name that is named.

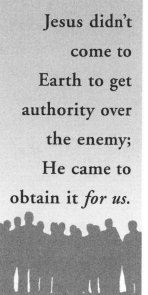

Jesus didn't come to Earth to get authority over the enemy; He came to obtain it *for us*.

YOU ARE HIS PEOPLE

You are His people. You are in Christ. You are the church of Lord Jesus Christ. You carry the glory and grace of God to everyone you meet—and nothing and no one can stop you.

> **And He put all *things* under His feet, and gave Him *to be* head over all *things* to the church, which is His body, the fullness of Him who fills all in all.**
>
> **Ephesians 1:22-23**

Paul begins this sentence with "And," because his prayer is not finished. He was just taking a breath.

Why is your life going to be different if you pray this over yourself for six months? No matter where you are or what you are doing, you will begin to realize that you are seated with Him at the right hand of your Father (Ephesians 2:6), and the "all things" under His feet are therefore under your feet. All of your issues and problems that you think are so big and overwhelming will look small and insignificant in light of what God has done and is doing in Christ.

All your fear and anxiety and confusion and anger get swallowed up in the exceeding greatness of His power toward you because you believe in Him and you are in His body. Instead of hanging your head in the back row of the church, thinking that being there is not really worth your time, you will hold your head up and listen because you know it's the *only* thing that is worth your time!

All this energy issues from Christ: God raised him from death and set him on a throne in deep heaven, in charge of running the universe, everything from galaxies to governments, no name and no power exempt from his rule. And not just for the time being, but forever. He is in charge of it all, has the final word on everything. At the center of all this, Christ rules the church. *The church, you see, is not peripheral to the world; the world is peripheral to the church.* **The church is Christ's body, in which he speaks and acts, by which he fills everything with his presence.**

Ephesians 1:20-23 MSG **(italics mine)**

If you turn on the television news, you can't help but recognize that the world thinks they are the center of everything that is happening. The devil has deceived them into believing something even he knows is not true. Even he knows that the church of Jesus Christ is the center of everything that is happening. The church is not peripheral to the world, the world is peripheral to the church! In other words: The most important decisions being made today are not being made in the White House or the courthouse; they are being made in the church house!

Remember Sodom and Gomorrah were not destroyed because of sin, they were destroyed because of a lack of righteousness. (Genesis 18 and 19.)

> The most important decisions being made today are not being made in the White House or the courthouse; they are being made in the church house!

YOU ARE HIS LIGHT

As one of God's people, you are His light in a dark world. That is your identity. Darkness (by definition) is the partial or total absence of light. In other words, the only hope darkness has to exist is if there is little or no light. When light is dim or gone altogether, the darkness prevails. However, when the light shines brightly, the darkness is completely removed.

> **In Him was Life, and the Life was the Light of men.**
> **And the Light shines on in the darkness, for the darkness has never overpowered it [put it out or absorbed it or appropriated it, and is unreceptive to it].**
> **John 1:4-5** AMP

Jesus is the Light, and we are in Him. The church is on the Earth today to shine His light, to reveal His redemptive truth and grace, so that the darkness is removed and people will come out of darkness and into the Light. Whatever happens in this world is directly related to what Jesus is doing—or is allowed to do—through His church.

> **Whatever happens in this world is directly related to what Jesus is doing—or is allowed to do—through His church.**

In 1909 a group of sixty church leaders in Germany met to debate and then write the Berlin Declaration. This document basically stated there was only one Day of Pentecost, and that was in Acts, chapter 2. Therefore, they declared that the Pentecostal Movement—which included speaking in tongues, the gifts of the Spirit, and manifestations of the Spirit such as falling under the power of God, shaking, weeping, or shouting—was the work of Satan, not God.

Of the sixty clergymen attending this meeting, all but four signed the Berlin Declaration. Afterward, slowly but surely, the light of the Gospel began to go out in Germany. The life and power of God left the Christian churches, and in 1933 an Austrian named Adolf Hitler became chancellor. In less than a generation the people who had rejected a move of God, calling it the work of Satan, put a man in power who proved to be an instrument of Satan. Not only did he commit genocide against the Jews by murdering over six million of them, he also murdered over three million Christians. In the pursuit of world domination, beginning in Europe, he destroyed his own country.

Our enemy's whole purpose is to snuff out the light and power of God's people so that no man, woman, or child can see Jesus and believe. Only a powerful church, built on the revelation of who Jesus is, will push back the gates of Hell to increase God's inheritance, His saints. The Bible says it is those of us who are in Christ who give hope to the world by shining His light and dispelling the darkness. We must not let His light in us grow dim! We must allow Him to shine brightly through us at all times!

In the middle of the gross darkness and depravity of mankind, Noah built an ark to the saving of his soul. He fulfilled the plan of God for his time right in the middle of that dark hour. Now, in our time, the church is the crowning achievement of the work of God in Christ. We are not an undercover group; Jesus declared we are a city set on a hill!

> **You are the light of the world. A city that is set on a hill cannot be hidden. Nor do they light a lamp and put it under a basket, but on a lampstand, and it gives light to all *who are* in the house. Let your light so shine before men, that they may see your good works and glorify your Father in heaven.**
>
> **Matthew 5:14-16**

We are not an undercover group; Jesus declared we are a city set on a hill!

Listening to the radio one day, I heard Paul Harvey say that he knew there was a

person listening to his voice who had a cure for a certain disease. He asked that person to call him and identify himself or herself. That is exactly what God is doing with you! He has called you out to assemble with His people, to grow strong in the power of His Word and His Spirit, and to be the light He created you to be.

I feel as if God is saying, "It's time you identified yourself. You are in Christ. You are My church, a city set on a hill and the light of the world. Stop hiding your light under a basket! Let your light shine to all who are in the house—and by the way, you have to be *in the house!* Get in the house I have set you in. Be a member of My body. Be part of My family. Then your light will always burn bright because you will find out what I am doing, how I am going to work through you, and you will see My ability in you multiplied by those you work alongside. I promise you that the light of My Son will shine through you like you could never have imagined."

IF YOU MISS THE VISION, YOU MISS YOUR TIME

Do you understand the significance of your life today?

Habakkuk 2:3 says, "The vision is yet for an appointed time." In other words, time and vision go together. If you miss the vision, you'll miss your time and you won't understand what God is doing during your lifetime today. The mystery of the church was revealed right on time – God's time. It wasn't hidden *from* you; it was hidden *for* you. It was only hidden so it could be revealed at the right time, which happens to be ...your time.

The mystery of the church came right on time—God's time. It wasn't hidden *from* you; it was hidden *for* you.

ERAS OF TIME

By faith we understand that the worlds [during the successive ages] were framed (fashioned, put in order, and equipped for their intended purpose) by the word of God, so that what we see was not made out of things which are visible.

Hebrews 11:3 AMP

I like the *Amplified Translation* of this verse because it conveys the true meaning of "worlds." This word doesn't mean planets or galaxies; it means "successive ages," specific periods of time that mark the history of mankind. This includes decades, centuries or millenniums. The Greek word translated "worlds" is *aion,*[1] which is where we get the English word, "eon." Have you ever heard anybody say, "It took eons and eons of time?" Well, that's the idea.

Although it is true that the physical universe was created by the Word of God, look at what follows Hebrews 11:3: "By faith Abel...By faith Enoch...By faith Noah...By faith Abraham...By faith Sarah..." (Hebrews 11:4-11). These all represent different people in different periods of time in which God worked to accomplish His purpose. These people were all significant simply because they embraced God's Word during their lifetime. This is what gave them a place in the eternal record of God's Word.

Now faith is the substance of things hoped for, the evidence of things not seen. For by it the elders obtained a *good* testimony.

Hebrews 11:1-2

The *New American Standard Bible* says that by their faith, "men of old gained approval." *The Message* says, "The act of faith is what distinguished our ancestors, set them above the crowd." These people were famous for their faith then, and they are famous for their faith now!

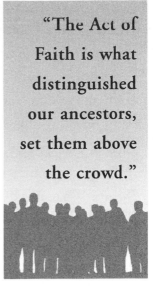

"The Act of Faith is what distinguished our ancestors, set them above the crowd."

During their specific periods of time they took a word from the Lord and upon His instructions rearranged, repaired, and made ready for its intended purpose the time they were living in. These people took what God said to them, lived it out by faith, causing it to change not only their lives, but also their generation.

HOW NOAH UNDERSTOOD HIS TIME

Acts 17:26 says that God determined the borders of the place in which you are living and the time in which you are living. You may have been an accident to your parents, but God knew you were coming! He foreordained that you would fulfill His plan for your life simply by receiving a word from Him. What changes a mess into a masterpiece? A word from God! Just read Genesis 1. Darkness and chaos covered the Earth, but one word from God completely transformed our planet.

You have to understand that God thinks dispensationally. He has a divine purpose to dispense in each age, and He dispenses His divine purpose through His people. How? By giving His people a

word. You could receive one word from Him like, "You are to build a boat," and your whole life would be set on a course that would cause your generation to come in line with God's redemptive plan for mankind. One word from God will give you a joy to persevere in the worst and the best of times.

Noah wouldn't quit even though everybody ridiculed him. If people weren't yelling at him, most likely they were saying cruel things about him under their breath. "What are you doing, old man? What are you doing out there, putting board after board on that boat? What's the matter with you? You're crazy, that's what you are!" They made fun of him. They ridiculed him. They said all manner of evil about him. They told him he was living a worthless, pointless life.

Hebrews 11 says the world was not worthy of Noah or of any of our heroes' faith because it could not understand them. The world of unbelievers does not "get" faith in God and His Word. Without being born again, they have no spiritual sight. But it didn't matter to Noah if the world accepted him or understood him. He was set in his position to preserve the redemptive plan of God in his generation, and he refused to come off of his watch. He wouldn't quit because he knew that what he was doing wasn't his idea. He did not give himself to a purpose or plan he had designed for himself.

Some people get all wrapped up in their own ideas about what should be or what shouldn't be. But building a boat wasn't Noah's idea; it was God's idea. Then it became Noah's idea. Genesis 6:8 says, "But Noah found grace in the eyes of the Lord." The fact that he found it means he must have been looking for it! There was so much evil in the people all around him, he was probably crying out to God for His grace and mercy. He must have been praying, "I know You can do something. I don't know what You are going to do; but when I find out, that is what I am going to do too."

Anyone who has put their faith in the Lord and is seeking Him will have a sense of when He is going to move in a tremendous way. Noah had never experienced a flood, but he knew the evil of his generation demanded a righteous solution. He knew God was going to do something. When God told him to build the ark and put all those animals on it, that gave Noah a clearer picture of what was about to happen.

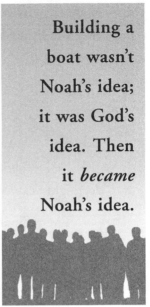

Building a boat wasn't Noah's idea; it was God's idea. Then it *became* Noah's idea.

In the same way, as you build the ark God has called you to build, working with the people He has called you to serve, you will get a clearer picture of what God is doing to reveal His glory and redeem His people in your time.

JUST ONE WORD WILL DO IT

Rick Renner, a noted Bible teacher, provides an expanded translation of Hebrews 11:2 based on the meaning in the original Greek:

Through unrelenting, never-give-up, bulldog faith, a faith that never lets go, we understand that different time

periods and different ages in past human history have been radically altered and changed by those who received and stood by a word from God.

If that doesn't light your fire, your wood's wet! I'm referring to the miracle that God did for Elijah in the Old Testament.

Elijah is another example of a man who knew what God wanted to do in his time, and that understanding empowered him to do mighty exploits for God.

> Then Elijah said to the people, "I alone am left a prophet of the LORD; but Baal's prophets *are* four hundred and fifty men. Therefore let them give us two bulls; and let them choose one bull for themselves, cut it in pieces, and lay *it* on the wood, but put no fire *under it;* and I will prepare the other bull, and lay *it* on the wood, but put no fire *under it.* Then you call on the name of your gods, and I will call on the name of the LORD; and the God who answers by fire, He is God."
>
> 1 Kings 18:22-24

Elijah set up a contest between God and Baal, and the whole idea was to see who was more powerful. The prophets of Baal went first.

> So they took the bull which was given them, and they prepared *it,* and called on the name of Baal from morning even till noon, saying, "O Baal, hear us!" But *there was* no voice; no one answered. Then they leaped about the altar which they had made.

And so it was, at noon, that Elijah mocked them and said, "Cry aloud, for he *is* a god; either he is meditating, or he is busy, or he is on a journey, *or* perhaps he is sleeping and must be awakened." So they cried aloud, and cut themselves, as was their custom, with knives and lances, until the blood gushed out on them. And when midday was past, they prophesied until the *time* of the offering of the *evening* sacrifice. But *there was* no voice; no one answered, no one paid attention.

1 Kings 18:26-29

This was pretty funny! The prophets of Baal did everything they could think of to get their demon god to show everyone how superior he was, but he did absolutely nothing. Then it was Elijah's turn to call on God.

Then with the stones he built an altar in the name of the LORD; and he made a trench around the altar large enough to hold two seahs of seed. And he put the wood in order, cut the bull in pieces, and laid *it* on the wood, and said, "Fill four waterpots with water, and pour *it* on the burnt sacrifice and on the wood." Then he said, "Do *it* a second time," and they did *it* a second time; and he said, "Do *it* a third time," and they did *it* a third time. So the water ran all around the altar; and he also filled the trench with water.

1 Kings 18:32-35

Elijah made it as easy as he could for Baal, allowing those prophets to do anything they could to get their god to respond

with fire. But he made it seemingly impossible for God to respond with fire by drenching the altar and the sacrifices with water not once, but three times! What happened?

> And it came to pass, at *the time of* the offering of the *evening* sacrifice, that Elijah the prophet came near and said, "LORD God of Abraham, Isaac, and Israel, let it be known this day that You *are* God in Israel and I *am* Your servant, and *that* I have done all these things at Your word. Hear me, O LORD, hear me, that this people may know that You *are* the LORD God, and *that* You have turned their hearts back *to You* again."
>
> Then the fire of the LORD fell and consumed the burnt sacrifice, and the wood and the stones and the dust, and it licked up the water that *was* in the trench. Now when all the people saw *it,* they fell on their faces; and they said, "The LORD, He *is* God! The LORD, He *is* God!"
>
> 1 Kings 18:36-39

Having faith in one word from the Lord turned the entire nation of Israel back to God!

I always tell people, "Listen, if your wood's wet, God can light your fire! Did you know God could light a fire with water? He can light wet wood!" What is humanly impossible is still possible with God, and through the years I have seen that this is something He loves to do again and again. How does He do it? The same way He did it for Elijah when Elijah declared, "You *are*

God in Israel and I *am* Your servant, and *that* I have done all these things at Your word."

Having faith in one word from the Lord turned the entire nation of Israel back to God! Elijah *framed his time* with God's Word. He was empowered and his own faith was set on fire by knowing what God wanted to accomplish in his generation.

GOD'S SUSTAINING WORD

I believe God can do what needs to be done even in our generation to turn things around. If He did it with Elijah and all the saints in Hebrews 11, then He can do it with us! We are not facing anything different than Elijah faced in his time. The prophets of Baal, the devil, and all his demons are still here doing the same false signs and wonders, deceiving people with half-truths, and leading the ignorant down paths of destruction. Any optimism or hope they give people is based on lies and illusion, but we are established and sustained by God's infallible Word.

Did you know the only true source of optimism and hope in your generation is people who have faith in God and His Word? The only people that will sustain any generation are those who know God and trust in His Word. People of faith! There are many who see the power of the faith of the

> The only people that will sustain any generation are those who know God and trust in His Word. People of faith!

143

saints and try to piggyback on their ideas of faith by secularizing the truth of God's Word. They don't want to get to the Father through the blood of Jesus (John 14:6). If they talk about Jesus, they present Him as a wise man, but not the God-Man. They turn the truth of faith in God and His Word into "human motivation," "the power of positive thinking," or any number of feel-good, self-help programs that resurface again and again, making the talk show rounds every few years. They have different names and catch phrases, but they all bend the truth in the same deceptive ways.

If you have become involved with a pseudo-spiritual movement or concept that is based on anything other than what God's Word says, I will tell you right now that you are standing on a platform that has a false bottom. As soon as the devil hits that mark on the back of your head, you are going to fall flat through all the lies you are standing on, and none of those religious ideas and spiritual philosophies are going to save you. Only the Word of the Living God will save you.

The Noahs and Elijahs of today don't fall for any of this stuff, and they are not popular around those who do! When you are like the heroes of faith in Hebrews 11 and stand on the Word of the Lord you have received for your life, it doesn't matter how many times the devil tries to make you sink or what people say about you, nothing can move you from your place in your generation because Jesus Christ, the Living Word, is your foundation.

The Word of God and the Word of the Lord for your time are an incredible combination of empowerment. They give you a determination that makes it impossible for you to quit. It doesn't matter what happens because before you ever have a problem, you already have the Answer. The Answer was given before the problem ever showed up!

Without meditating on the specific word of God for your life and studying His Word you will probably not consider what you will do when trouble comes. You will wait until a problem shows up and say, "Now what am I going to do? Am I going to serve God, am I going to believe God, am I going to speak the Word? I don't know if I am going to do it this time. Maybe I should sit this one out."

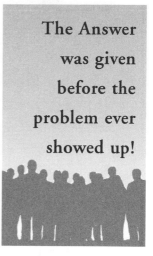

The Answer was given before the problem ever showed up!

Remember, we talked about the fact that to be preplanned is to be prepared. The heroes of faith were prepared because they had already planned what they would do during the good times and during the bad times. When a bad time hits you, it is not a good time to decide whether or not you are going to stick with God and His plan. You are making your decision at the wrong time because you are more likely to quit when the price to continue is high.

I know there are some people who have to have a challenge before they really make up their minds to serve God no matter what, but I wouldn't recommend it! Believers who know their time and God's plan for their time are more likely to choose to serve Him regardless of the difficulties and obstacles. They make up their minds from the moment God says, "This is your part in My strategic plan for your time. This will reveal My saving grace for your generation." They decide to see this through regardless of their circumstances or how people treat them.

That is what Jesus did. In the Old Testament, speaking of Jesus, Isaiah 50:6-7 KJV (italics mine) says, "I gave my back to the smiters, and my cheeks to them that plucked off the hair: I hid not my face from shame and spitting. For the Lord GOD will help me; *therefore shall I not be confounded: therefore have I set my face like a flint*, and I know that I shall not be ashamed." When Jesus faced being falsely accused, beaten, scourged, mocked, and crucified, He was not confounded. He wasn't confused, caught off-guard, or surprised in any way. He had set His face like a flint. He had determined ahead of time that nothing would move Him away from God's will for His life and His time, which was to bring forth His church.

> **We are to live with our end in mind; we should decide what we are going to do today based on where we want to end up.**

Psalm 90:12 tells us to ask the Lord to teach us about the time we are living in so we can have a heart of wisdom to make the right decisions. Most people live from what's right in front of them. They make value decisions and set their standards when they face whatever life throws at them. God's people are not to live that way. We are to live with our end in mind; we should decide what we are going to do today based on where we want to end up. That's how we walk by faith, fulfilling our part in God's plan for our time by standing on the Word of God.

THE BOOK OF ACTS IS YOUR TIME

We've seen how Noah and Elijah and all the heroes of faith in Hebrews 11 were empowered in their time. Now it's your time to be empowered!

In the book of Acts, you read how people like the Apostle Paul carried out their part in God's strategic plan. When they were baptized in the Holy Spirit on the Day of Pentecost, they received the help and power necessary to be the instrument of change during this hour. They did it by establishing, strengthening and helping the local church, through which Jesus would then reveal the universal church. Well, Christian, we are still living in the Book of Acts!

Today, during the time that you and I are living in, God is continuing to change history through the lives of those who hear and obey His Word. This is the Church Age, where Christians are called together in the local church for a purpose that is greater than that of any one individual. As we grow in the Word of God, are changed by the Spirit of God and connected with the people of God, there will be a witness to the world of the saving, healing, and delivering power that raised Christ from the dead!

> **Christians are called together in the local church for a purpose that is greater than that of any one individual.**

WHERE IS JESUS TODAY?

In recent years I have heard a lot of believers say, "Well, you know, if Jesus were on the Earth today He wouldn't be in church. He'd be out on the streets. He'd be at the marketplace." Now I'm all for street evangelism and going to the highways, byways, our offices, and our workplaces to bring people into the kingdom of God, but this kind of statement leaves you with the impression that Jesus is not interested in the local church today. Even worse, it implies that He is through with the local church, that it has become an outdated, spiritually dead institution.

To say that God is finished with the church is one of the most ungodly, devilish things one could ever say. Jesus lived, died, rose again, and is coming back for the church! People who say these things have not read their Bible. They need to read through the book of Acts and the Epistles to see the vital importance and impact the local churches had back then. Then they need to take a look in the book of Revelation and see where Jesus is today.

JESUS IS STANDING IN OUR MIDST

There are many scriptures that say Jesus rose from the dead, ascended to Heaven, and sat down at the right hand of the Father; but there are only two times after He ascended that the Bible says Jesus was standing up.

The first time Jesus stood was when Stephen was stoned to death.

> **But he, being full of the Holy Spirit, gazed into heaven and saw the glory of God, and Jesus standing at the right hand of God, and said, "Look! I see the heavens opened and the Son of Man standing at the right hand of God!"**
>
> **Acts 7:55-56**

To say that God is finished with the church is one of the most ungodly, devilish things one could ever say. Jesus lived, died, rose again, and is coming back for the church!

What a picture of absolute, final power and authority. When Jesus stands up at the right hand of the Father for you, you know everything is going to be more than all right! It doesn't matter what you are going through or how you feel because He has the final word about you and your life.

The other time Jesus was standing is found in the book of Revelation, written by the Apostle John when he was in exile on the Isle of Patmos.

I was in the Spirit on the Lord's Day, and I heard behind me a loud voice, as of a trumpet, saying, "I am the Alpha and the Omega, the First and the Last," and, "What you see, write in a book and send *it* to the seven churches which are in Asia: to Ephesus, to Smyrna, to Pergamos, to Thyatira, to Sardis, to Philadelphia, and to Laodicea."

Then I turned to see the voice that spoke with me. And having turned I saw seven golden lampstands, and in the midst of the seven lampstands *One* like the Son of Man, clothed with a garment down to the feet and girded about the chest with a golden band.

He had in His right hand seven stars, out of His mouth went a sharp two-edged sword, and His countenance *was* like the sun shining in its strength. And when I saw Him, I fell at His feet as dead. But He laid His right hand on me, saying to me, "Do not be afraid; I am the First and the Last."

Revelation 1:10-13,16-17

When Jesus walked the Earth, John was probably the closest person to Him; and yet when Jesus appeared to him—and John even said he was "in the Spirit"—he fell down like a dead man. If you wonder why people fall under the power of God in church, it is because that which they have been spiritually born into becomes more real than the natural world. Their place in Christ Jesus is more real to them than their natural mind can fathom. When that happens, they just can't stay on their feet!

These verses in Revelation are speaking to our day. Jesus is involved in the activities of our local churches in this hour. John was seeing a current event, and this was not like a newspaper; it was the Living Word of God. A newspaper is new in the morning and old in the evening, but the Word of God is Eternal—and it is always true. His Word never fails, and it is never out-of-date. It is a current event for every time, and now Jesus the Living Word is right in our midst.

> *One* like the Son of Man, clothed with a garment down to the feet and girded about the chest with a golden band. His head and hair *were* white like wool, as white as snow, and His eyes like a flame of fire; His feet *were* like fine brass, as if refined in a furnace, and His voice as the sound of many waters.

Revelation 1:13-15,18

A newspaper is new in the morning and old in the evening, but the Word of God is Eternal—and it is always true.

Wool is an emblem of eternity and spotless purity. His eyes are flames of fire, piercing through everything, reflecting His omniscience. His feet are as bright as polished bronze, denoting strength and stability, as if they had been fired in a furnace until they were completely refined—and they are still red hot! His voice thunders like the mighty ocean waves. This is a voice that brings overwhelming comfort to His own, but terror to His enemies. No one would dare talk back to someone with such a voice!

I am He who lives, and was dead, and behold, I am alive forevermore. Amen. And I have the keys of Hades and of Death.

Revelation 1:18

> His very presence cries out, "It doesn't matter what adversity you are facing. I have purchased for you an eternal victory, and I'm standing right in the middle of your church with it!"

Jesus' feet are still red hot because He has personally walked through all your trials and tribulations. He has walked right through all your sins and the consequences of your sins: death, Hell, and the grave. Now His feet are burning—not with the fires of Hell but with the fire of God, the resurrection power that brought Him out of the tomb and set Him at the right hand of the Father. His very presence cries out, "It doesn't matter what adversity you are facing. I have purchased for you an eternal victory, and I'm standing right in the middle of your church with it!"

The devil doesn't have an answer for that kind of voice. That's the kind of voice the church speaks with in this hour, a voice that roars like thunder because the Author and Finisher of our faith is in us and in the midst of us. The gates of Hell shall not prevail against us because Jesus is standing among us!

John knows this is Jesus, but Jesus is no longer the suffering servant. He has fulfilled that part of God's plan. Now He is the King of kings and Lord of lords, He has conquered death and Hell,

all things are under His feet and He has a revelation for the Apostle John that involves seven letters to seven *local churches*.

JESUS IS WALKING AROUND THE LAMPSTANDS

Write therefore the things you see, what they are [and signify] and what is to take place hereafter.

As to the hidden meaning (the mystery) of the seven stars which you saw on My right hand and the seven lampstands of gold: the seven stars are the seven angels (messengers) of the seven assemblies (churches) and the seven lampstands are the seven churches.

Revelation 1:19-20 AMP

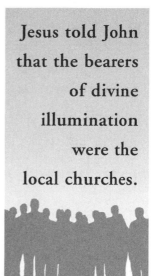

Jesus told John that the bearers of divine illumination were the local churches.

In John's time a lampstand was a tall, oil-burning lamp. It was a type of the Holy Spirit and the light of God's Word that give us divine illumination in this dark, fallen world. Jesus told John that the bearers of divine illumination were the local churches. He is reminding John of something He taught the disciples before His death.

You are the light of the world. A city set on a hill cannot be hidden.

Nor do men light a lamp and put it under a peck measure, but on a lampstand, and it gives light to all in the house.

Let your light so shine before men that they may see your moral excellence and your praiseworthy, noble, and good deeds and recognize and honor and praise and glorify your Father Who is in heaven.

Matthew 5:14-16 AMP

> Your light will only shine as bright as your commitment to your local church because the local church is where the light of Jesus shines!

Your light will shine brightest when you commit to the local church. The next time you go to church, just ask the Holy Spirit to open your eyes so you can see Jesus walking in your midst. Church will never be the same! You may not see Him physically, but you will always see Him as He reveals Himself in all His glory through you and your brothers and sisters in Christ.

I promise you, it will change your idea of what "having church" is all about and why you are gathering together. The revelation that you get from the book of Revelation is that Jesus is in the local church today. Furthermore, if you read His letters to the seven local churches in Revelation 2 and 3, you will see that He knows everything that is going on in our churches and has specific instructions for each individual body of believers. If you're not there you will miss what He's saying to you!

If you want to receive specific instructions concerning your Commander-in-Chief's strategy on the Earth today, you have to be in your place in your church because that is where Jesus is

speaking to His people. He reveals His battle plans and gives instructions for every area of your life, as well as for the church-at-large, in the local church. He will use the five-fold ministries and other members to speak to you, correct you, equip you, encourage you, and show you His plan for you in the context of your local assembly and His entire body. Most of all, He will give you someone to watch over your soul.

> He reveals His battle plans and gives instructions for every area of your life, as well as for the church-at-large, in the local church.

THE STARS IN JESUS' RIGHT HAND

Jesus tells John that the seven lampstands are the seven churches, but He also tells him about the seven stars. Jesus holds these stars in His right hand, which is a symbol of

authority, and He calls these stars "angels." The Greek word translated angels is *aggelos*, but it means more than just angels. One scholar's definition of *aggelos* is, "A messenger, one who is sent in order to announce, teach, perform, or explore anything. The angels of the seven churches are probably the bishops or pastors of those churches."[1]

Most teachers and scholars agree that the seven stars are pastors because other verses of Scripture indicate that pastors shepherd the sheep in the local church. They watch over our souls. They keep us moving in the right direction with the right heart attitude. Most importantly, they feed us the Word of

> Most teachers and scholars agree that the seven stars are pastors because other verses of Scripture indicate that pastors shepherd the sheep in the local church.

God—that two-edged sword that is coming out of Jesus' mouth, the message for the hour in which we are living. Your pastor is the one who preaches the Word of God to you 'up close and personal'! He's the one who answers your questions, discerns how you are doing, and prays for you.

In Acts 20:17 Paul called a meeting of the elders of the church at Ephesus. The word "elders" indicates they were those "to whom was committed the direction and government of individual churches."[2] Paul was about to go to Jerusalem, where he would encounter great trials. He knew he would never see these brothers again.

When someone is giving their last words to you, the last words you will ever hear them say on Earth, you know they are important. This is what Paul said to them:

I have not shunned to declare to you the whole counsel of God. Therefore take heed to yourselves and to all the flock, among which the Holy Spirit has made you overseers, to shepherd the church of God which He purchased with His own blood. For I know this, that after my departure savage wolves will come in among you, not sparing the flock. Also from among yourselves men will rise up, speaking perverse things, to draw away the disciples after themselves.

Therefore watch, and remember that for three years I did not cease to warn everyone night and day with tears.

Acts 20:27-31

In essence, Paul told these leaders, "Make sure you pastor the church of God because this act of pastoring the flock is the sustaining and protecting power of the move of God in this hour. When the pastor preaches and teaches the whole counsel of God, the flock of God will not fall prey to wolves and false leaders who come in to carry them into the ways of darkness."

Pastoring a church is a mighty calling. No wonder Jesus holds the leaders of the churches in His hands like stars!

PASTORS SHOW YOU THE RIGHT WAY

You need a pastor to keep you from being confused and discouraged, not knowing where you are going or why. Proverbs 29:18 says, "Where there is no vision, the people perish." *The Message* says: "If people can't see what God is doing, they stumble all over themselves." Flipping channels one day I caught about five minutes of the Jerry Springer television show, and I thought, *That is Proverbs 29:18 right there! Those people are stumbling all over themselves. They have no vision, no knowledge of God, and no understanding of what God is doing today.*

The *New American Standard Bible* says it this way, "Where there is no vision, the people are unrestrained." This gives us a picture of people who have no direction. They have no inner ability to restrain themselves from doing stupid and self-destructive

things because they have no fellowship with God or His people. They have no leader to lead them and no local body of believers to encourage them to restrain their flesh and walk in the Spirit and the Word of God.

Being under the care of a pastor gives you understanding about what God is doing today from His Word and by His Spirit. A pastor puts Godly borders around your life and imparts Godly vision, giving you the strength to keep yourself from being distracted or led astray by selfish desires or false doctrines.

Good pastors understand that God's strategic plan for today is not about trying to find something new; it is hooking up with what's true.

See to it that no one takes you captive through philosophy and empty deception, according to the tradition of men, according to the elementary principles of the world, rather than according to Christ.

Colossians 2:8 NASB

Good pastors understand that God's strategic plan for today is not about trying to find something new; it is hooking up with what's true. They know that by staying with what's true, even if you've heard it a hundred times before, it becomes newer and more powerful to you. Your pastor may repeat a message from last year, but you hear it and see it in a way you never have before. The Holy Spirit adds another dimension to the gift God has placed in your life or opens up a deeper dimension of a simple revelation. He's not really doing anything new, but it's fresh every day, like manna from Heaven.

Jesus uses pastors to build His church upon the fundamental principles of biblical truth, namely, who He is, what He has done, and what He is now doing through His church. They may use unique and creative methods to illustrate the new birth, for example, but the methods must reinforce the principal truth that Christ died for our sins and rose from the grave to give us a new life, a life free from the bondage of sin and death and all the power of the devil.

I read somewhere that America consumes more medication for insomnia and depression than any country in the world. The churches in America offer the only real cure: the Living Word of God. His name is Jesus, and the only side effects are righteousness, peace, and joy in the Holy Ghost! A person can be in the same home with the same family and have the same job at the same company as they were before they got saved, but everything looks different after they have been forever transformed by Jesus on the inside. He turned on the light! That is the power of our salvation in Jesus Christ.

I read somewhere that America consumes more medication for insomnia and depression than any country in the world. The churches in America offer the only real cure: the Living Word of God. His name is Jesus, and the only side effects are righteousness, peace, and joy in the Holy Ghost!

WHO IS YOUR PASTOR?

For more than thirty years of ministry, we have always made one thing very clear: We are not pastors! Nor do we want to pastor those on our mailing list. Our role as a ministry gift is to serve and assist the pastors in their crucial calling in the body of Christ. Understanding this truth will not only bring an increase to itinerant ministries, it will also bring healthy fruit to their ministries.

> Our role as a ministry gift is to serve and assist the pastor in their crucial calling in the body of Christ.

Some traveling ministers and television ministers don't want to hear that. In fact, there are some on television who actually give the impression that the purposes of God would be accomplished if people considered them their pastor, their broadcast as their church service, and sent their tithe to them. In light of what we have read in the Word of God concerning Jesus' commitment to and involvement in the local church, this is just not supported by Scripture. It is also totally impractical. It is this kind of teaching that diminishes the work of Jesus through His body.

I've got nothing against television ministries or ministries that hold city-wide meetings, as long as they don't try to take the place of the local church. They have a place, but they cannot take the place of the local church. Furthermore, the local church needs your financial support as they bring Jesus into your neighborhood every day. As much as we enjoy and need the ministry of our favorite teacher or televangelist, none of them can fulfill the unique, dynamic role the pastor has in our lives.

The Pastoral office is not an occupation. It is an anointed gift for the church and that anointing is best received in a face-to-face, here-and-now meeting in the local assembly. You can't get the same impact from the television or radio. Who will go through the joys of life with you? Who will marry you and bury you? Who will counsel you when you are confused? Who will visit you or your family if you are in the hospital? Who will be there to bring comfort to you or your family when you lose a loved one or feel like the bottom just dropped out of your life? Your pastor, that's who!

Your pastor is one of the greatest gifts God gives to you. No one else can take his place!

> The Pastoral office is not an occupation. It is an anointed gift for the church and that anointing is best received in a face-to-face, here-and-now meeting in the local assembly.

WHAT ABOUT THE OTHER MINISTRY GIFTS?

And He Himself gave some *to be* apostles, some prophets, some evangelists, and some pastors and teachers, for the equipping of the saints for the work of ministry, for the edifying of the body of Christ,

Ephesians 4:11-12

Speaking of Jesus, Ben Campbell Johnson translates Ephesians 4:12 like this: "He acts through these special functions to enable the members of the family to fulfill their mission, which will in turn enrich the entire body of Christ."[3] You need the other ministry gifts in order to grow up in God, but these gifts are to strengthen the local church.

What other ministry gifts say about the local church is important. If you are called as an apostle, prophet, evangelist, or teacher, you must be careful not to diminish the local church by implying you or others don't need it. If you desire God's anointing upon you so you can stand effectively in your place, you must understand what your place is and what your place is *not*. You are not the shepherd of the sheep, and you must be careful never to discount or undermine the man or woman who is called of God to fulfill that responsibility and assignment.

Without a pastor, the fruit produced by the other ministry gifts can't be sustained.

When other ministry gifts leave the impression that people don't need the local church, they are also implying that people don't need a pastor. This causes a great hindrance to the work of God. Without a pastor, the fruit produced by the other ministry gifts can't be sustained. The seed planted will lie dormant, receiving no water or sun, and producing no lasting fruit.

All sheep need a shepherd or they will grow hardened to the things of God. When they are first saved their hearts are tender, but without the encouragement and loving guidance of a pastor, their hearts slowly grow insensitive to the Word and the Spirit. God has anointed the local church, and particularly the gift of the pastor, to ensure this doesn't happen.

When other ministry gifts recognize this, they should support the local churches and pastors. Their own ministries will grow and thrive because when they come to town, the believers there will be hungry for what they have to impart. Their hearts will not have grown cold. Other ministry gifts who support the pastors and local churches where they minister will grow and flourish because they are also being a part of God's strategic plan for our time.

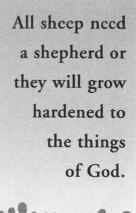

All sheep need a shepherd or they will grow hardened to the things of God.

WHAT ABOUT WORLDWIDE EVANGELISM?

When you talk about world evangelism, you are talking about a function of the local church. Every person who accompanied the Apostle Paul on a missionary journey was a part of and was known by the local church. Real evangelism begins *and ends* in the local church. Jesus told us we were to make disciples not converts (Matthew 28:19). If an evangelist never connects with a local church, his big evangelistic meeting is actually going to hinder—not help—the plan of God because it will cause people who don't have a pastor to be confused and scattered.

Then Jesus went about all the cities and villages, teaching in their synagogues, preaching the gospel of the

kingdom, and healing every sickness and every disease among the people. But when He saw the multitudes, He was moved with compassion for them, because they were weary and scattered, like sheep having no shepherd.

Matthew 9:35-36

We don't want people to scatter either! We want to *gather* them to the local church to be nurtured and cared for as they grow up in Christ. Discipleship is the work of the local church. You cannot effectively disciple someone without a Pastor and the supernatural functioning of the body of Christ in a local church, where they can grow in the things of God as they live out the plan of God.

Some years ago we were getting ready to travel to Paris, France, to do a conference. We got an e-mail from a man representing a large church there who did not know anything about us. He asked us not to come if we were just going to do another big crusade and then leave. That would not help them. They needed a ministry that would strengthen the churches because after we left town, it was the churches that would determine how far the move of God would go.

We answered by giving them the link to our website so they could look at our materials and know our purpose in coming to

> Every person who accompanied the Apostle Paul on a missionary journey was a part of and was known by the local church. Real evangelism begins *and* ends in the local church.

Paris. We told them our mission statement: "Strengthen the church—reach the world." We wanted them to understand that we believe the only way to reach the world for Jesus Christ and make disciples of the nations was to strengthen the local churches. We tell people all the time, "We don't have a ministry that stands alone; we are a ministry to the local church." We don't have any reason to exist without you! What we see

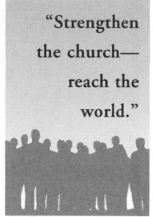

"**Strengthen the church— reach the world.**"

from the Word is that if we were to try to function apart from the local church, we simply would not be able to effectively fulfill our role in God's plan for today.

KNOW THEM!

And we beseech you, brethren, to know them which labour among you, and are over you in the Lord, and admonish you.

1 Thessalonians 5:12 KJV

Personally, if I was a pastor, I would never have a ministry gift in my church who wasn't a member of a local church, and by that I mean firmly connected to and known by their pastor and their congregation. To me, this says they personally are on track with Jesus and what He is doing today. If they aren't a part of a local church, the danger is that they won't understand the function and significance of the local church, so they will not know how to properly administer their gift. They will see it as separate and possibly superior to the ministry of the local church and pastor.

Pastors are more apt to trust a ministry gift who says, "Just call my pastor. He'll tell you all about me." If anyone wants to know about us, they can call our pastor and he will tell them. He is our shepherd, and we are so grateful God put us under his care in our local church. We can be "partners" with other ministries, but there is only one place where we are "members," and that is our local church. We are a part of that particular body and family.

> We can be "partners" with other ministries, but there is only one place where we are "members," and that is our local church.

Although we hear lots of messages as we travel around the world, the most powerful Word we hear comes from our pastor. Jesus holds him in His hand, and He always has our pastor say just what we need to hear! Furthermore, although we are encouraged by many around the world, there is nothing like coming home and being with our church family. They are the ones who are there for us through thick and thin. We know our relationship with our pastor and our local church is one of the keys to our success in life and ministry.

You are greater with other believers than you are by yourself, and you need a shepherd to watch over your soul. You need a pastor to bolster your faith and help you to do your part in completing God's plan for your time, someone who will bring in other ministry gifts to equip you for the work of the ministry and keep you on the right path. You need someone who knows you and whom you know.

JESUS IS PREPARING YOU

Jesus is walking among the lampstands and holding the stars in His right hand today. He is preparing us so that we can accomplish what He wants to accomplish, and He is preparing us for the last days of the Church Age which are upon us right now!

The closer we get to the end of the Church Age, the more important this preparation becomes. Rick Renner translates 2 Thessalonians 2:1:

> **Brothers, I make this urgent, heartfelt request to you today, earnestly and sincerely pleading with you from the bottom of my heart to hear what I'm telling you and to do exactly as I say. The appearance of the Lord Jesus Christ is very near. In fact, it is so close that we can nearly feel His presence as if He were already here among us.**

(That reminds me of Jesus walking in the midst of our churches!)

> **The moment we have all longed and waited for is almost upon us! I'm talking about that moment when Jesus will finally gather us together for Himself.**

The focus here is on how urgent and short our time is. Paul believes the Church Age is quickly coming to an end, and he is begging us to wake up and complete the mission God has given us for our generation.

If you want an interesting study, read through the book of Revelation and note how many times Jesus says He is coming quickly. In Revelation 3:11 He says, "Behold, I come quickly." *The Message* says, "I'm on My way; I'll be there soon." In Revelation

22:7 He says, "Behold, I am coming quickly!" And in Revelation 22:12, "And behold, I am coming quickly, and My reward is with Me." I like what the Word says in Revelation 22:20: "He who testifies to these things says, 'Surely I am coming quickly.' Amen. Even so, come, Lord Jesus!"

Throughout the book of Revelation Jesus is telling us that time is winding up. He's preparing us for what is about to happen, but He is also warning us that we don't have much time left to accomplish His purpose. Rick Renner continues his expanded translation of 2 Thessalonians 2:2:

> Some things will be happening right before His coming that could shake you up quite a bit. I'm referring to events that will be so dramatic that they could really leave your head spinning, occurrences of such a serious nature that many people will end up feeling alarmed, panicked, intimidated, and even unnerved! Naturally speaking, these events could nearly drive you over the brink emotionally, putting your nerves on edge and making you feel apprehensive and insecure about life.
>
> I wish I could tell you these incidents were going to be just a one-shot deal, but when they finally get rolling, they're going to keep coming and coming, one after another. That's why you have to determine not to be shaken or moved by anything you see or hear. You need to get a grip on your mind and refuse to allow yourselves to be traumatized by these events. If you let these things get to you, it won't be too long until you're a nervous wreck! That's why you have to decide beforehand that you are not

going to give in and allow fright to penetrate its way into your mind and emotions until it runs your whole life.

In order for you to remain strong and to fulfill your part in God's strategic plan for today, you must always be mindful that Jesus is standing right in the middle of your church. When you are alone, you can easily think He has abandoned you; but in the company of your brothers and sisters it is easy to know He has neither left you nor forsaken you. He is there, telling you, "Let not your heart be troubled!"

After calming the saints in 2 Thessalonians 2:1-2, Paul goes on to warn them about what's coming. Again, here is Rick Renner's expanded translation of 2 Thessalonians 2:3:

> In light of these things, I urge you to refuse to allow anyone to take advantage of you. For example, you won't need a letter to tell you when the day of the Lord has come. You ought to know by now that this day can't come until first a worldwide insurgency, rebellion, riot, and mutiny against God has come about in society.

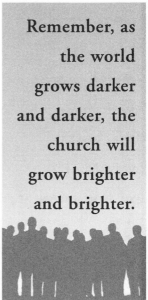

Remember, as the world grows darker and darker, the church will grow brighter and brighter. The ones you are praying for are going to see that light because the darker it gets, the brighter the light of Jesus will shine through you and your local church. The atmosphere in your church

Remember, as the world grows darker and darker, the church will grow brighter and brighter.

will be completely different than on the streets or in a coffee shop, and the corporate anointing of believers will powerfully affect a person's response to God during these times.

Just as John the Baptist was given a mandate from Heaven to prepare the way for the first coming of the Lord, the church has been given the mandate from Heaven to prepare the way for His second coming.

Hebrews 10:25 says, "Not forsaking the assembling of ourselves together, as *is* the manner of some, but exhorting one another, and so much the more as you see the Day approaching." I believe that the assembling of believers in these last days is integral to His Second Coming. Just as John the Baptist was given a mandate from Heaven to prepare the way for the first coming of the Lord, the church has been given the mandate from Heaven to prepare the way for His second coming.

In fact, the Word of God has a lot to say about our role in these last days. Continuing with Rick Renner's expanded translation of 2 Thessalonians 2:3-6:

> Once that occurs, the world will then be primed, prepared, and ready to embrace the Man of Lawlessness, the one who hates law and has rebellion running in his blood. This is the long-awaited and predicted Son of Doom and Destruction, the one who brings rot and ruin to everything he touches. When the

time is just right, he will finally come out of hiding and go public!

Do you understand who I am talking about? I'm describing that person who will be so against God and everything connected with the worship of God that, if you can imagine it, he will even try to put himself on a pedestal above God Himself sitting in God's rightful place in the temple and publicly proclaiming himself to be God!

Don't you remember that when I was there with you, I used to regularly tell you these things?

Now in light of everything I've told you before, you ought to be well aware by now that there is a supernatural force at work, preventing the materialization of this person and the disclosure of his identity. This restraining force I'm referring to is so strong that it is currently putting on the brakes and holding back the unveiling of this wicked person, stalling and postponing his manifestation.

What is that supernatural restraining force? The body of Jesus Christ! When I read this, I know this time is not the enemy's time; this is our time! We are the ones who push back the darkness, defeat the enemy at every turn, and bring multitudes to the saving knowledge of Jesus Christ our Lord. Ours is not a story of doom and gloom and no hope.

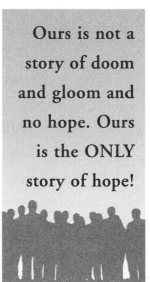

Ours is not a story of doom and gloom and no hope. Ours is the ONLY story of hope!

Ours is the ONLY story of hope! We carry in our hearts and in our churches the only hope for the world. Our story has the only real "happily ever after" ending because it ends in the glory and honor and power of the Living Lord (Revelation 4:9,11; 19:1, 21:24).

The Bible says it is the glory of God, *"Christ in you,"* that gives hope to the world and fills it with light, the light that shines through and dispels the darkness (Colossians 1:27). The greatest move of God's Spirit to save, heal, deliver, set free, and to bring forth signs, wonders, and miracles is happening right now, and it is happening in and through local churches all over the world.

What did Jesus say about the church in Matthew 16:18-19 KJV? He said, "The gates of hell shall not prevail against it. And I will give unto thee the keys of the kingdom of heaven: and whatsoever thou shalt bind on earth shall be bound in heaven: and whatsoever thou shalt loose on earth shall be loosed in heaven." You are not trying to *get* victory. You already have it! You got victory before you ever had the problem. Jesus prepared the way for you, and that means you are prepared.

You are prepared to restrain the enemy.

You are prepared to repel every lie and deception the world throws at you and hurl the absolute truth of the Living God right back in their faces.

You are prepared to fulfill the part you were created for in God's strategic plan for today when you take your place in the local church.

THE ANSWER TO A NATION'S PROBLEMS—HISTORY IS HIS STORY

> **God, who at various times and in various ways spoke in time past to the fathers by the prophets, has in these last days spoken to us by *His* Son, whom He has appointed heir of all things.**
>
> Hebrews 1:1-2

Every age before the Church Age spoke of and pointed to the first coming of Jesus and hinted at the mystery of the church. Jesus came, and now God is speaking to the world through His body, His witness on the Earth. When we view history through the eyes of God, we can easily see that in every era of time He had someone to speak for Him. Today it is His church.

> The strength of any nation is dependent on the strength of the church of Jesus Christ, and that translates into the strength of the local churches.

The strength of any nation is dependent on the strength of the church of Jesus Christ, and that translates into the strength of the local churches. In the early 1830s a Frenchman named Alexis de Tocqueville came to America to examine its civil institutions. He was astonished to see that although the American people were quite religious, they were also free. He wrote:

> The Americans combine the notion of Christianity and liberty so intimately in their minds that it is impossible to make them conceive the one without the other...
>
> There is no country in the whole world in which the Christian religion retains a greater influence over the souls of men than in America...its influence is most powerfully exercised over the most enlightened and free nation of the earth.[1]

In de Tocqueville's France and in any secular form of government today, people believe religion inhibits freedom. If you don't have religion, then you will be free. The idea is that there won't be any oppressively imposed values or standards of behavior. Let each person determine their own beliefs, behavior, and purpose. As long as no one bothers anyone else, everyone will be free. This, of course, is foolishness when you know the truth of God's Word. Separated from the Father, human beings are fallen and sinful—not just against Him, but also against each other. The Ten Commandments alone tell the full story of how we destroy each other!

> **Righteousness exalteth a nation: but sin is a reproach to any people.**
>
> Proverbs 14:34 KJV

God's truth is that freedom from sin is the source of all other freedoms, and peace with God in the hearts of people will produce peace in all human relationships. Also, freedom from sin was bought and purchased by the shed blood of Jesus Christ. It came with a price! Our nation's founders knew this and most of them lived by this truth. That's why they were willing to fight for what they believed.

During the French Revolution of 1789, the rebel leaders cracked down on the Church, confiscating its property and bringing all clergy under control of the state. The Cathedral at Notre Dame was rededicated to the Cult of Reason and the altars were desecrated. In 1792 they did away with the annotation A.D. (Anno Domini, or "the Year of our Lord"), and declared that year to be "Year One" of their republic without God. What followed was anarchy and then tyranny. In Paris, more than 20,000 were killed in what became known as the Reign of Terror.

> God's truth is that freedom from sin is the source of all other freedoms, and peace with God in the hearts of people will produce peace in all human relationships.

Alexis de Tocqueville grew up in the aftermath of the French Revolution and Napoleon Bonaparte years. He was fascinated by different cultures and governments, and he came to America to find the source of its greatness. Where did he find it?

> I sought for the greatness and genius of America in her commodius harbors and her ample rivers and it was not there.

Alexis de Tocqueville found in America the secret of freedom and liberty for all: The Gates of Hell could not prevail against the church— the true church of Jesus Christ.

I sought for the greatness and genius of America in her fertile fields and bounteous forests and it was not there.

I sought for the greatness and genius of America in her rich mines and her vast world commerce and it was not there.

I sought for the greatness and genius of America in her public school system and her institutions of learning and it was not there.

I sought for the greatness and genius of America in her democratic congress and her matchless constitution and it was not there.

Not until I went into the churches of America and heard her pulpits aflame with righteousness did I understand the secret of her genius and power.

America is great because America is good and if America ever ceases to be good, America will cease to be great.[2]

Alexis de Tocqueville found in America the secret of freedom and liberty for all: The Gates of Hell could not prevail against the church—the true church of Jesus Christ. The tyranny, terror, and darkness that had covered France through the Revolution of 1789 could have been prevented had true believers been practicing a real Christianity in the churches there.

Do you see why the devil wants us to believe that going to church every Sunday and mid-week is no big deal? He tells us the lie that singing in the choir, volunteering at the food and clothing ministry, going to the hospital to pray for the sick, ushering people into the building with care, and getting our kids in Sunday school are not that important in the big scheme of things. I mean, if the economy is unstable and most of the government is filled with godless people, what difference is one little church going to make?

Jesus, the Bible, *and history* all tell us the devil is a liar!

WE ARE ON DISPLAY

The church is the divine instrument of God's strategic plan for this hour. Jesus demonstrates His redemptive work, the power of His cross and resurrection, through

> Nations do not fall into the hands of the enemy and go dark because people *outside* the church refuse to move with God; nations fall into the hands of the enemy and go dark because God's people *inside* the churches refuse to move with Him.

His body. Nations do not fall into the hands of the enemy and go dark because people *outside* the church refuse to move with God; nations fall into the hands of the enemy and go dark because God's people *inside* the churches refuse to move with Him. When the church is truly the body of Christ to its generation, righteousness exalts that nation and throws out the powers of darkness.

To me who am less than the least of all God's people has this work been graciously entrusted to proclaim to the Gentiles the Good News of the exhaustless wealth of Christ, and to show all men in a clear light what my stewardship is. It is the stewardship of the truth which from all the Ages lay concealed in the mind of God, the Creator of all things concealed in order that *the Church might now be used to display to the powers and authorities in the heavenly realms the innumerable aspects of God's wisdom.*

Ephesians 3:8-10 Weymouth (italics mine)

Do you want to know what your purpose is right now? You are to display the "manifold wisdom of God" to all the angels and demons. Why? The war between God and Lucifer, who became Satan the adversary of God, has been won by Jesus Christ the Son and we are in Him for the express purpose of revealing that victory to all who have participated in this war. We are to demonstrate the victory of Jesus Christ over all the power of the enemy.

Through the ages God has said to Satan, "Look at My servant Job. Isn't he amazing? Look at My servant Abraham, up there on

Mount Moriah, getting ready to sacrifice his only son for Me. Look at My servant David, who's taking Jerusalem and bringing peace to My people Israel. And NOW, look at My Son Jesus and His body, My church. The gates of Hell are crumbling everywhere they assemble together and make disciples of the nations!"

We are not only on display to the angels and demons; we are also on display to the people around us. Second Corinthians 6:1,3-4 MSG says,

> "Companions as we are in this work with you, we beg you, please don't squander one bit of this marvelous life God has given us…. People are watching us as we stay at our post, alertly, unswervingly…in hard times, tough times, bad times."

W. O. Carver's paraphrase of Ephesians 3:10 says,

> "This plan and method God adopted and carried out in order that now through the presence and faithful functioning of the Church, which he is creating and in which his grace is manifested, the many-sided wisdom of God may be made known to the ordered systems of rule and authority in the heavenly realms. For indeed the history of our race on earth may well appear as a contradiction of God's wisdom and a denial of His righteousness, until it is interpreted in the achievement of redemption by the Christ through His Church."[3]

This paraphrase gives a different view of the same truth. The entire history of mankind will seem like it contradicts God's wisdom and denies His righteousness if the church does

> When the church ceases to be the church on a local level, reaching out to and impacting communities with the saving grace of the Gospel, believers lose their identity, purpose, and any concept of what God is doing in their time.

not make known and demonstrate who it is in Christ Jesus. All of history becomes distorted and perverted when the church does not function as the body of Christ. Human beings lose real historical perspective when they view history apart from the knowledge of Jesus and His church because all of God's people in preceding ages prepared for, looked for, and led up to the Church Age!

When the church ceases to be the church on a local level, reaching out to and impacting communities with the saving grace of the Gospel, believers lose their identity, purpose, and any concept of what God is doing in their time. Unbelievers have no picture of Jesus or the Father to look at, and they just throw up their hands and say, "I don't even know why there are churches. I don't see any evidence of God. I don't even see any hope for the future." The world around us is waiting for our churches to show them the truth and the hope only Jesus can give them.

Throughout America's history, local churches that were asleep have awakened to this understanding, and they changed the course of our history.

WE MUST KNOW THE HOUR

Besides this you know what [a critical] hour this is, how it is high time now for you to wake up out of your sleep (rouse to reality). For salvation (final deliverance) is nearer to us now than when we first believed (adhered to, trusted in, and relied on Christ, the Messiah).

The night is far gone and the day is almost here. Let us then drop (fling away) the works and deeds of darkness and put on the [full] armor of light.

Romans 13:11-12 AMP

But make sure that you don't get so absorbed and exhausted in taking care of all your day-by-day obligations that you lose track of the time and doze off, oblivious to God. The night is about over, dawn is about to break. Be up and awake to what God is doing! God is putting the finishing touches on the salvation work he began when we first believed. We can't afford to waste a minute, must not squander these precious daylight hours in frivolity and indulgence, in sleeping around and dissipation, in bickering and grabbing everything in sight. Get out of bed and get dressed! Don't loiter and linger,

> When you recognize that God has set you in an historical moment, a sense of change resonates in your spirit and begins to permeate the atmosphere around you.

181

waiting until the very last minute. Dress yourselves in Christ, and be up and about!

Romans 13:11-14 MSG

We need to open our eyes and recognize the season and the opportunities God has given us. When you recognize that God has set you in an historical moment, a sense of change resonates in your spirit and begins to permeate the atmosphere around you. You carry with you the "anything is possible with God" anointing, always hinting at a moment of opportunity, of turning things around.

As God's partners, we beg you not to accept this marvelous gift of God's kindness and then ignore it. For God says,

"At just the right time, I heard you. On the day of salvation, I helped you."

Indeed, the "right time" is now. Today is the day of salvation.

2 Corinthians 6:1-2 NLT

But this I say, brethren, the time *is* short, so that from now on even those who have wives should be as though they had none, those who weep as though they did not weep, those who rejoice as though they did not rejoice, those who buy as though they did not possess, and those who use this world as not misusing *it*. For the form of this world is passing away.

1 Corinthians 7:29-31

All of these verses refer to the immediacy of our call from God for today. The *Amplified Bible* says, "The appointed time has been winding down and it has grown very short." *The Message* says, "There is no time to waste, so don't complicate your lives unnecessarily."

You say, "He doesn't want me to get married?" No, Paul goes on to say in 1 Corinthians 7:32-35 MSG, "I want you to live as free of complications as possible... I'm trying to be helpful and make it as easy as possible for you, not make things harder. All I want is for you to be able to develop a way of life in which you can spend plenty of time together with the Master without a lot of distractions." He wants the saints to have plenty of time to spend together with the Master. That's the local church!

All Paul is saying is that he wants us to keep our priorities straight. We must always view our marriages and children and jobs and even our ministries in light of the urgency of our time. Going to church shouldn't be last on our list. It must be a top priority because that is how God is moving in our time and the time is short!

THE GREAT AWAKENING

In the 1730s, life in colonial America was hard, and one war after another discouraged many who had come here for a better life and religious freedom. There was a shortage of churches and ministers, and many Christians had no spiritual care or fellowship with other believers. Overall they were sheep without shepherds, and they were scattered.

At this time a pastor in Northampton, Massachusetts, named Jonathan Edwards came to prominence. He felt the spiritual deadness throughout the land and decided to pray to God for revival. In 1733 a revival broke out. It spread through the Connecticut River Valley, and the news of it reached England and Scotland, bringing great preachers like George Whitfield to America. By 1739 it was called the Great Awakening, and it changed the course of America.

The Great Awakening transformed the entire nation's spiritual and moral character by winning the lost and establishing local churches with the life of God in them.

The Holy Spirit poured out significantly in Northampton. It was reported that the entire town had an awesome sense of the presence of God. Jonathan Edwards wrote:

There was scarcely a single person in the town, old or young, left unconcerned about the great things of the eternal world...

Our public assemblies were then beautiful: the congregation was alive in God's service, everyone intent on the public worship, every hearer eager to drink in the words of the minister as they came from his mouth; the assembly were in general from time to time in tears while the word was preached; some weeping with sorrow and distress; others with joy and love, others with pity and concern for the souls of their neighbors.[4]

People came to Northampton from other towns with great skepticism, but there was such an overwhelming presence of the Spirit of God in the city, they would end up being saved and dramatically changed. Then they went back to their own towns and churches and the awakening spread. How did it spread? As they went out from the local church! The Great Awakening transformed the entire nation's spiritual and moral character by winning the lost and establishing local churches with the life of God in them.

When George Whitfield preached in a church, the power of God would move through the congregation. What we know as manifestations of the Spirit happened during his meetings. He wrote, "Look where I would, most were drowned in tears. Some were struck pale as death, others wringing their hands, others lying on the ground, others sinking into the arms of their friends and most lifting up their eyes to heaven and crying out to God."[5]

From his other writings, we know Benjamin Franklin was not a believer, but he became a friend of George Whitfield. Being a journalist among other things, this is what Franklin wrote about him in his autobiography.

In 1739 there arrived among us from Ireland the Reverend Mr. Whitfield who made himself remarkable there as an itinerant preacher. He was at first permitted to preach in some of our churches, but the clergy, taking a dislike to him, soon refused him their pulpits, and he was obliged to preach in the fields. The multitudes of all sects and denominations that attended his sermons were enormous and, it was a matter of speculation to me, who was one of the number, to observe the extraordinary influence of his oratory on his hearers.

(That extraordinary influence Franklin observed was the anointing of the Holy Spirit!)

From being thoughtless or indifferent about religion, it seemed as if the whole world were growing religious so that one could not walk through the town in an evening without hearing psalms sung in different families of every street.[6]

Benjamin Franklin heard families of saints praising and worshipping God in their homes as he walked through the town. He and all the founding fathers of the United States of America were dramatically influenced by this revival.

The manifestations of the Holy Spirit these early American believers were experiencing are very familiar to us today, especially in the Pentecostal and Charismatic movements of the twentieth century and into this century. What they called "fainting," we call "falling under the power of God." Back then some people stayed at the meetings or in the church all night, lying there communing with God just like people do in some of our meetings today.

There arose opposition to these meetings, of course, in the churches and outside the churches. When the Spirit of God moves mightily in a time and place, it really rattles a lot of people's cages! They will either yield to the Spirit and be free of their cages or they will lock their doors even tighter. One of the people who decided to lock his door tighter wrote about his experience at a revival meeting.

> *These meetings would continue till 10, 11, 12 o'clock
> at night; in the midst of them sometimes 10, 20, 30 and
> sometimes many more would scream and cry out, or send
> forth the most lamentable groans, whilst others made great
> manifestations of joy by clapping their hands, uttering
> ecstatic expressions, singing psalms and inviting and
> exhorting others.[7]*

Another person who opposed the revival wrote:

> *The noise was like the roar of Niagara.
> The vast sea of human beings seemed to
> be agitated as if by a storm. Some of the
> people were singing, others praying, some
> crying for mercy in the most piteous
> accents, while others shouted vociferously.
> A strange supernatural power seemed to
> pervade the entire mass of mind there
> collected...At one time I saw at least five
> hundred, swept down in a moment as if a
> battery of a thousand guns had been
> opened upon them, and then immediately
> followed shrieks and shouts that rent the
> very heavens. I fled for the woods...and
> wished I had stayed at home.[8]*

Glory to God! If you don't have
something they don't have, they won't be
coming; but we *do* have what the world
wants. We've just got to let the Holy Spirit

The faith, courage, and passion that produced the United States of America and formed it into the great nation it became can be traced to the pulpits and pews of its local churches.

use us so they can see what He is convicting them of: they are sinners in need of our Savior, Jesus.

Many Americans became missionaries as a result of the Great Awakening, which spread to other countries. This move of God transformed the moral atmosphere of colonial America and re-established us as a Christian nation. What we now call the Ivy League colleges like Princeton, Harvard, and Columbia, were all begun primarily to train ministers of the Gospel. Harvard Professor William Perry said, "The Declaration of Independence of 1776 was a result of the evangelical preaching of the evangelists of the Great Awakening."[9]

The devil wants you to think that the local church is the most insignificant part of turning the tide in this hour. Why? Because he knows, and history bears this out, that the exact opposite is the truth! The faith, courage, and passion that produced the United States of America and formed it into the great nation it became can be traced to the pulpits and pews of its local churches. The freedom and liberty we prize so much were not political ideas; freedom and liberty were absolute truths founded in the redemptive work of Jesus Christ and planted in the hearts of believers all across this country in their local churches.

ARE YOU AWAKE NOW?

If we fail to focus on what He is doing today through the local church, we will wake up someday simply older and tired, saddled with regret for having missed the move of God for our time.

Recently I gave this word from the Lord:

So this is the day and this is the hour. Oh, the people of God are rising up with fresh power. No, it shall not be as it has been, for I've got a plan. It begins, and it has an end. And as you step forward in faith and belief, oh, you watch out! You watch out! Things will change that you thought could never be changed. It will work where it didn't work. It will go where it didn't go. It will rise where it fell. For I am the One who has given you this day, and I will stand and I will protect. That which I began shall surely be finished, and it shall be accomplished. Though you are weak, I am strong. Though you are small, I am great. Though you have limits, I have none. So rise up in strength, for this is your day!

God is raising up strong local churches today, filled with believers who are flowing in the power and fruit of the Holy Spirit. Local churches that will rise up, determined not to miss the move of God for our time, are the ones that are destined to make a difference in our generation.

This is our hour; this is our day! Jesus has made you a part of His supernatural body, the breadth and extent of whose faith and power have yet to be fully seen.

Embrace the mission as you take your place among the most powerful people on Earth, taking the message of the glorious Gospel to a world that so desperately needs a Savior.

Be confident, be steadfast and be unmoved, for the gates of hell *will not* prevail against the church of the Lord Jesus Christ—

Amen, and Amen!

ENDNOTES

1 You Are Here…

[1] For more study on the dispensations and ages, see Finis Jennings Dake, *Dake's Annotated Reference Bible* (Lawrenceville, GA: Dake Bible Sales, Inc., 1963), p. 59-62.

[2] http://www.studylight.org/isb/bible.cgi?query=dispensation&section =0&it=kjv&ot=bhs&nt=na&Enter=Perform+Search

[3] Spiros Zodhiates, *The Complete Word Study Dictionary: New Testament,* (Chattanooga, TN: AMG Publishers, 1992), #3622.

2 Your Divine Connection Reveals Your Divine Purpose

[1] James Strong, *Exhaustive Concordance of the Bible,* "Greek Dictionary of the New Testament," (Nashville, TN: Thomas Nelson Publishers, 1984), #1577.

[2] William Barclay, *New Testament Words* (Louisville, KY: Westminister John Knox Press, 1974), pp. 68-69.

[3] *Ibid.,* pp. 69-70.

6 Your Identity is in Him

[1] Kenneth S. Wuest, *Wuest's Word Studies in the Greek New Testament, Volume I,* "Ephesians" (Grand Rapids, MI: Wm. B. Eerdmans Publishing Company, 1973, 1983), pp. 53-54.

7 If You Miss Your Vision, You Miss Your Time

[1] James Strong, *Exhaustive Concordance of the Bible,* "Greek Dictionary of the New Testament," #165.

8 Where Is Jesus Today?

[1] Spiros Zodhiates, *The Complete Word Study Dictionary: New Testament,* #32.

[2] Ibid., #4245.

[3] Ben Campbell Johnson, *The Heart of Paul* (Waco, TX: Word Books, 1976), p. 128.

9 The Answer To A Nation's Problems
History is His Story

[1] Alexis de Tocqueville, *American Institutions,*" chapter xvii: http://books. google.com/books?id=MwvBo3kFsgoC&pg=PA31&dq=The+Americ ans+combine+the+notion+of+Christianity+and+liberty#PPA31,M1

[2] http://books.google.com/books?id=3sYpAAAAYAAJ&pg=RA3-PT21&dq=I+sought+for+the+greatness+and+genius+of+America

[3] W. O. Carver, *Ephesians: The Glory of God in the Christian Calling* (Nashville, TN: Broadman Press, 1949), p. 174.

[4] Most of the historical information on the Great Awakening, including the following quotations, are gratefully attributed to Eddie L. Hyatt, *2000 Years of Charismatic Christianity: A 21st Century Look at Church History from a Pentecostal/Charismatic Perspective* (Lake Mary, FL: Charisma House, 2002), p. 108-109.

[5] *Ibid.,* p. 110.

[6] *Ibid.,* p. 110-111.

[7] *Ibid.,* p. 112.

[8] *Ibid.,* p. 116.

[9] *Ibid.,* p. 112.

LIST OF BIBLE TRANSLATIONS

Unless otherwise indicated, all scripture quotations are taken from the *New King James Version*. Copyright © 1982 by Thomas Nelson, Inc. Used by permission. All rights reserved.

Scripture references marked MSG are taken from *The Message*. Copyright © by Eugene H. Peterson, 1993, 1994, 1995. Used by permission of NavPress Publishing Group.

Scripture quotations marked JPS are taken from *the JPS Old Testament (1917)* © 2000 by Larry Nelson, Box 2083, Rialto, CA 92376. All rights reserved. Used by permission.

Scripture quotations marked AMP are taken from the *Amplified® Bible*. Copyright © 1954, 1958, 1962, 1964, 1965, 1987 by The Lockman Foundation. Used by permission. (www.Lockman.org)

Scripture quotations marked KJV are taken from the *King James Version* of the Bible.

Scripture quotations marked NASB are taken from the *New American Standard Bible®*. Copyright © 1960, 1962, 1963, 1968, 1971, 1972, 1973, 1975, 1977 by The Lockman Foundation. Used by permission. (www.Lockman.org).

Scripture quotations marked NIV are taken from *The Holy Bible: New International Version®* NIV ®. Copyright © 1973, 1978, 1984 by International Bible Society. Used by permission of Zondervan Publishing House. All rights reserved.

Scripture quotations marked Weymouth are taken from the *New Testament in Modern Speech* by Richard Francis Weymouth. Copyright © 1978 by Kregel Publications, Grand Rapids, Michigan.

MEET THE AUTHOR—
BY CINDY DUVALL

It is an honor to introduce my most loyal friend and co-worker in the faith, Lois Taucher. She, her husband Ray, and I, have served in ministry together as Shekinah Glory since 1978, more than three decades at this writing. Lois' gifts as a teacher, preacher, vocalist, songwriter, and evangelist continually bring people from darkness into God's light and impart strength to the body of Christ.

Lois attributes her love for Christ and the church to her mother, who kept her and all of her siblings in church while they were living at home. The Father's gifting and calling on Lois' life became evident at the early age of nine, when she made Jesus the Lord of her life. As a young Southern Baptist, she experienced the fire of God and an aggressive and expressive faith. This early foundation thrust Lois into the Jesus Movement, and as a "Jesus hippie" she preached the message, "Turn or burn!"

Looking back Lois says, "I always knew I had a home in Heaven, but I never knew Heaven had a home in me." Because of this lack of understanding, the years that followed brought much heartache. She became a backslidden Christian, working in a nightclub. Even then, however, two things still remained in her heart: the fire of God and the passion to know Him.

I saw Lois for the first time in 1976. I had just returned from a USO tour and had been booked as a featured artist at a famous supper club in Nashville, Tennessee. Although I had a Jewish heritage, I was a backslidden Southern Baptist who had recently rededicated my life to the Lord. (Someday I'll write a book!) I walked into the club and saw nineteen-year-old Lois, serving drinks and cashiering. I passed her on my way to my dressing room and heard myself saying, "Lord, You have something for us to do."

The other waitresses told Lois that I had "gotten religion," and Lois said, "Well, I can handle religion." One evening she came into my dressing room and we began to talk. Out of the blue she said, "I don't like people who say praise the Lord, and I like to smoke."

I just said, "Okay." She was surprised I didn't jump on her. Later I heard she could sing, and I asked her to come up and sing with me. We had a great blend and started singing together regularly. Eventually, I asked her to church, and we sang together at church. We were two formerly backslidden believers trying to find our way in what God had called us to do.

After we had both moved to Tulsa, Oklahoma, my hometown, we met Ray at a radio telethon. He heard us sing and asked God if he could play guitar for us. We didn't know this, but that week we called Ray and asked him to come hear us sing at Grace Fellowship (now Grace Church). He came to hear us, and we have been singing and ministering together ever since. In 1989, after twelve years of ministry together, Ray and Lois married.

In 1980 we all graduated from Rhema Bible Training Center in Tulsa. Lois credits much of her spiritual growth to the teaching and instruction she received from Brother Kenneth E. Hagin, especially on our authority as believers, as well as the other teachers there. It was there she learned that Heaven had a home in her. The revelation of who she was in Christ brought forth the inner joy, peace, and stability she had always longed for in her walk with the Lord.

In our early years together we read through the book of Acts and saw how Paul went from place to place strengthening the local churches. We knew that was what God had called us to do. Then, the day after the September 11, 2001, attacks on the United States, God spoke clearly to Lois, "Build My Church." The teaching contained in this book is what God put in her heart, what she has taught and preached and lived in front of me through our years together.

Today Lois continues to move forward with the same passion for all God wants to do in her and through her. She lives *God's Strategic Plan for Today*, which are the words of Jesus to Peter in Matthew 16:18: "I will build my church, and the gates of hell shall not prevail against it."

To introduce such a woman of integrity, honesty, and a love for Jesus Christ and the local church to you is a privilege and a joy.

—Cindy Duvall
President and Founder
Shekinah Glory Ministries

ABOUT SHEKINAH GLORY MINISTRIES

Shekinah Glory is a unique ministry team set within the church to stir up and strengthen believers in their understanding of the Gospel of Jesus Christ. Since establishing the ministry in 1978, Cindy Duvall, along with Lois and Ray Taucher have continued to be obedient to their heavenly commission.

As a traveling ministry, Shekinah Glory has made the strengthening of the local church their main focus. They believe the most effective means of reaching the world with the Gospel of Jesus Christ is the local church. Toward that end each of them effectively inspires by living a life of faith, and together they reach out to sinners with God's hand of grace. The result of this emphasis is "fruit that remains."

Cindy, Lois, and Ray consider it a privilege to be God's ambassadors. They have ministered in nineteen nations and have focused much of their missionary efforts in France. In the early 1990s they began co-hosting an annual ministers' conference in the South of France, and today they host an annual ministers' conference in Paris. They believe the answer to the turmoil in today's world is the presence and influence of strong local churches in every community.

With that in mind they fan the flame of revival in the lives and ministries of local congregations, setting hearts on fire to become all God has called them to be. Many miracles confirm the power of the Gospel as burdens are removed, chains are broken, the sick

are healed, and the captives are set free! One pastor said, "They don't just sing, they don't just teach—they change your life forever because they *impart.*"

Shekinah Glory Ministries offers other products to aid in your spiritual growth. For a complete list of teaching series, music CD's, and books, or to request our quarterly newsletter or view our podcasts and daily devotions on our website, please contact us at the appropriate address or call us.

Shekinah Glory Ministries, Inc.
P. O. Box 33108
Tulsa, OK 74153
918-250-1227

Via e-mail at:
<u>shekoffice@aol.com</u>

Visit our website:
<u>www.shekinahglory.com</u>

In Canada, you may contact our Canadian Office:
Shekinah Glory Ministries, Inc.
P.O. Box 4, Station Central
Red Deer, Alberta, T4N 5E7
403-340-3946

We would like to gratefully acknowledge all of those whose contributions helped make this book a reality...

Pastors Edwin and Angela Anderson
Pastors Larry and Judy Bjorklund
Jeanne Bowser
Gerald and Marie Cantalupo
Pastors Richard and Corrine Cardoza
Larry and Beverly Jean Coffey
Pastor Tom and Connie Cromwell
Vincent Cupolo
Jerry and Kathryn Estes
William and Twyla Fettis
Stan and Linda Folsom
Karl and Carol Fricke
Janet Gantz
Pastor John and Ingrid Huizing
Robert Andrew and Rachel Jenkinson
Ray and Sally Martin
Pastors Bill and Fredna McNeese
The Montelone Family
Mark and Cathy Redwine
Pastors Rick and Denise Renner
The Sicilia Family
Susie Tregoning
Hurshel and Dorothy Whitehurst
Larry and Bevery Willige
Nancy and Tadeus Winiecki
Robert and Denise Wraight
Canada Word of Faith Ministries
Grace Church
Redeeming Love Christian Center
And
All the Partners and Friends of
Shekinah Glory Ministries

As a pastor and a traveling minister, I have seen lots of distractions about the local church and its purpose. With this book, Lois puts the local church back into its right place: the center of what God is doing. Lois brings the reader back to the heart of God's Will for our generation and the generations to come. This book's teaching has dramatically changed our understanding of what God is looking for from us as a local church and should be in the hand of every pastor.

Pastor Donato Anzalone, Living Word Christian Center,
Lugano, Switerzland

I have had the privilege of experiencing Lois Taucher's ministry many times over the years. Lois is a gifted teacher with a message that will stir you up and get you excited about being a vital part of the your local church. Her insight and simplicity allow the Word of God to speak directly to your heart and energize your walk with Him.

Pastor Stanley L. Moore Sr., Words of Life Church,
North Miami Beach, Florida

Lois' unrelenting commitment to the local church is evident. What is most impressive is how, after over 30 years of traveling ministry, the passion and fire for the church is still so obvious both in words and practice.

Pastor Emory Goodman, Cliffdale Christian Center,
Fayetteville, North Carolina

Powerful! Practical! Provoking! A must-read for every believer and every pastor. This book will ignite you to speedily get into your place in a local church, and be a part of God's bigger plan for your life, your city, nations and the world.

Pastors Bracken and Donna Christian,
Family Harvest Church, Lubbock, Texas
Co-Founder of Family Harvest Church of Post,
Plainview & Seminole Texas

Lois Taucher is one of the most gifted Bible teachers I have ever known. Lois' clear and precise method of teaching will captivate the reader as revelation and understanding concerning God's purpose for the local church flows out of the pages of this book.

Pastor Ed Taylor, Faith and Victory Church,
Greensboro, North Carolina

Shekinah Glory has widened, enriched our vision of the local church and our daily walk with the Lord Jesus: we gained more boldness, hope and confidence in the One to whom nothing is impossible.

Yannick ANDRE, Eglise Protestante Evangelique de Cergy-Centre, CERGY-PONTOISE (Paris area), FRANCE

You will be changed from 'one glory to another' as you apply the truths that she so aptly presents. It is our great privilege to highly recommend to you her book *Called Together.*

Pastors Tim and Charmaine Phillips, Grace Christian Center, Harrison, Arkansas

The excellence and the power of Lois Taucher's message comes from the fact she sees the Church in its glory! The revelation that she has received on the Church is inspiring and liberating; this book is an essential tool for each of us.

Pastor Monique Sebilleau, Centre d' Evangélisation Revivre, Vichy, France

I believe this book will dispel the myths of people's pre-conceived ideas of 'church' and enlighten and strengthen their appreciation for one another and the One who fills all and is in all!

Rev. Daphne Delay, Pastor-Teacher, Family Harvest Church, Seminole, Texas

Every Pastor should have this book. It is scriptural, informative, and very important to the church. I know that Lois supports and knows the position and responsibility of the local church.

Pastor Lee Morgans, A Glorious Church, Collinsville, OK

Lois, thank you for not compromising the move of the Holy Spirit, and showing us that we are a supernatural church, called to do supernatural works.

Pastor J.C. Neff, Grace Family Church, Effingham, IL

Lois Taucher preaches the greatest message on the local Church that I have ever heard! This is a 'need-to-read' for every shepherd and every sheep.

Pastors Kevin and Heather Sanford, Abundant Life Center, Galway, Ireland

We first heard Lois teach when Shekinah Glory visited our church in 1985 and have received from her ministry many times over the years. When she shared this message with our church, people were challenged, encouraged, and changed.

Pastors Willie and Laura Dueck, New Beginnings Family Church,
Calgary, Alberta Canada

Understanding the truth of the church 'not being peripheral to the world but the world being peripheral to the church' has transformed my view to *God's* view of His design for the church.

Pastors Craig and Sharon McCune,
New Creation Church, Salt Lake City, Utah

In this age of casual relationships and fear of commitment, God's people need to come to a true understanding of what the Church is. Lois Taucher has a fresh message filled with powerful truth that will challenge <u>all</u> believers to grow up and wake up. 'Called Together' is a 'NOW' word from God that's been like fire shut up in her bones. It is a must-read for all those who want to see the Church Victorious.

Pastor Larry Millis, Living Word Family Church,
St. Joseph, Illinois

Lois Taucher is a dynamic Christian whom I have known for many years. As the body of Christ we have been *Called Together* to do great exploits. Be inspired and challenged as you read and assimilate the truths contained in this book.

Pastor Rick Moore, Words of Life Church,
North Miami Beach, Florida

Believers who lay hold of these truths and apply them to their lives will inevitably develop their God-given potential to fulfill their personal role within the local church, strengthening the church body as a whole, enabling it to carry out the Great Commission.

Pastor T.L. Sadler, 'R' Church, Madison, Wisconsin

It is refreshing to not only read God's revelation on the printed page, but also, to know that the author has experiential knowledge of the truth taught. Lois hits a 'home run' in both ways.

Pastor Gary L. Voss, The Bridge Community Church,
Winter Haven, Florida

Lois Taucher removes the shroud of speculation and confusion that has plagued the hearts of believers as it pertains to the local church's purpose, its importance to God Himself, and the great glory that God has ordained His church to walk in. Thank you, Lois, for shedding light on subject that has lived in the shadows; you have brought to the forefront truths that will cause the local church to walk in the glory that God intended.

Pastor Sterling Hudgins, Agape Family Church,
Manhattan, Kansas

In the few years that I have had the opportunity to know Lois she has been a huge blessing in my life! She has such a heart for ministers, believers and the whole church corporately...

Pastor Matt Flanders, Lebanon Family Church, Lebanon, Missouri

I have been a children's minister for 38 years; the children are tomorrow's leaders and the local church is the backbone for building strong Godly families. Thank you for this book!

Gloria Hancock, Children's Minister, Melody Christian Center,
Live Oak, Florida

Lois Taucher has marvelous revelation about the local church and its significance in these last days. Her teaching has been inspirational as well as informational to me.

Pastor Bert Phagan, Praise Center, Brussels, Belgium

Having pastored a church for nearly 30 years, I can attest to the fact that Shekinah Glory Ministries has always been a breath of fresh air, having ministered in our church more times than we can count. Their heart of love for the local church is unprecedented with a pure heart of ministry toward the Pastor, his immediate family, and congregation. This book by Lois Taucher is their heart, pure and simple. AWESOME!!

Pastor Marlon Sparks, Victory Family Church, Perryton, Texas

I believe the insight to the church that Lois Taucher has can enhance the church to a degree never seen before. I recommend this book to the entire body of Christ.

Pastor Jerry Piker, Opened Door Christian Fellowship,
Sunrise Beach, Missouri

Lois' book is timely. We need to return to the importance Jesus meant for the local church. Thank you, Lois, for obeying God.

Pastor Darrell Morgan, Word of Life Church, Apopka, Florida

"As a pastor, Lois's teaching on the local church is so needful and refreshing! This teaching, along with her presentation, makes these truths desirable to all. You will want this book to take top shelf in your library!"

Pastor Danny Bauer, Work of Faith Family Church,
Lander, Wyoming

Through insightful teaching, she unveils the role of the church in our lives, and explains the value and eternal benefits every believer can partake of by being a part of a local church.

Pastor Peggy Heald, Believer's Victory Church,
Lake Worth, Florida

In *Called Together*, Lois Taucher expresses so accurately what every Pastor wants his congregation to know regarding the role of the local church and its importance in the Plan of God.

Pastor John and Ingrid Huizing, Family of Faith Church,
Red Deer, Alberta, Canada

Lois exhibits a cry that thunders from the heart of Shekinah Glory Ministries. This book is a must for all pastors and those in leadership. Lois, we salute you for your meditation, determination and diligence in writing this book. May God use this book to start a revival in the heart of man. To God be the glory!

Pastors Scott and Maureen Stanek,
Bastrop Christian Outreach Center, Bastrop, Texas

Lois Taucher has a tremendous amount of revelation on the subject of the local church, a revelation the entire body of Christ needs today.

Pastor Gary Kruzan, Faith Christian Family Church,
Rushville, Illinois

Many in the Body of Christ are believing God for a great Outpouring. The proper foundation must be laid. Having ministered in local churches, large and small, in over 18 countries around the world,

Lois Taucher is anointed and uniquely equipped to bring us this message. The release of this book is God's perfect timing!

Harold and Peggy Cagle, WOFR.ORG
Word of Faith Internet Radio

We have known Lois and Shekinah Glory for 30 years. The subject of Christ and His church is one of her main topics. This book will bless and strengthen the local body.

Pastor W. A. Gorman, New Life Outreach, Danville, Arkansas

We are living in the last days and it is vital that the body of Christ knows they are the triumphant church. This is a book that will definitely be a blessing to every member of the body of Christ.

Pastor Stan Moore, Jr., Words of Life Church,
North Miami Beach, Florida

This book will help you to see that the local church is the place for continual light to bring people together, drive back fear, eliminate confusion and to declare through each individual member that 'His' church, 'His' body is alive and doing quite well!

Pastor David Leggett, New Life Fellowship, Council Bluffs, Iowa

I highly recommend Lois Taucher's new book on the local church. This teaching will be a blessing to pastors and to those called to serve the vision of their pastor!

Pastor Stan Pody, Faith Christian Center, Ruston, Louisiana

Everything Jesus is doing today, He is doing in and through the church. We found our identity, our purpose, and our future all in the church. Lois has a revelation of the church and it's purpose on Earth. Find your place - it's all in the church!

Pastors Ronnie and Kathy Pittman, Glory Tabernacle,
Asheville, North Carolina

Lois beautifully reveals the truths that make it possible for everyday people to supernaturally both lead others and participate themselves in the body of called-out believers known as the Church.

Pastors George and Carol Kearns, Lighthouse Word Church,
Chiefland, Florida

Every believer will benefit from reading this book by Lois Taucher. Lois does an outstanding job of teaching on the importance and the power of the local Church in every generation.

Mark and Trina Hankins, Teacher / Evangelist,
Alexandria, Louisiana

Lois's teaching on the local church is a blessing. I have heard her speak and her insights are a great asset to any pastor wanting to strengthen his commitment from the congregation.

Pastor Bob Yandian, Grace Church, Tulsa, Oklahoma

The message of the significance and vital importance of the local church to the plan of God is something that believers must be taught in this hour. A lack of knowledge of this very thing has weakened the church and kept us as a whole from being the powerful influence in the earth God intended us to be. Our prayer is that this book would travel around the world and that it's message would be welcomed, received and acted upon. We highly recommend this book to every leader, minister and believer.

Kevin and Susan Fletcher,
Living Word Global, UK and Ireland

In this book, the Church of the Lord Jesus Christ, the thing nearest His heart, is held high with the honor it deserves. With poetic grace, solid scholarship and the timely power of a prophet's voice, Lois Taucher chases away unsettling thoughts and restores the vision and boldness all of us need to persevere and accomplish our work in these last days. What a friend we've found—in Jesus, and in His gift to the Body of Christ.

Pastor Loren L. Hirschy, Word of Life Church, DuBuque, Iowa

It is time for each member of the Body of Christ to be in their place. Lois' book will play a vital role in achieving this, because it is filled with information and instructions for the body to go forward. As Lois has said, "The church is God's divine strategy for today!" You don't want to pass up the opportunity to meld yourself into this teaching concerning the church!

Pastor Arcie Brown, Life Fellowship Church,
Bowling Green, Kentucky

Having known Lois for many years and having had Shekinah Glory minister at our church a number of times, I can say she is one the finest Bible teachers I have ever met, with a strong anointing and heart for the local church.

Pastor Anthony Storino, Abundant Grace Church,
Toms River, New Jersey

We have known Lois Taucher since 1980. Lois stands in the office of a teacher and has used her gift to present biblical truth and understanding of the Local Church and its place in the plan of God. This is a timely book for all, pastors as well as everyone in the Body of Christ.

Pastors Richard and Corrine Cardoza, The Lord's Church,
Sacramento, California

This book establishes the importance of the Pastoral Ministry; it underlines the necessary synergistic cooperation between the five Ministries within the Local Church, and the unique and essential place of each believer in the Body of Christ. This message will cause any believer to think twice before ever leaving the local Church!

Pastor Babeth Chorel, Eglise Siloe, Malissard, France

Lois has received supernatural revelation into the great mystery concerning Christ and the Church. This message will help position the local church for this last-day move of God.

Pastor David Hodges, Family Worship Center, Gulfport, Mississippi

There is nothing more important in this day of harvest than strong, passionate local churches who understand their place as Jesus' light in this world. I believe this message is a catalyst which will bring change wherever God's people are assembled together.

Toni Haskell, Missionary, Manila, Philippines

God's plan for mankind and for each individual is directly linked to the local church. This book is a must for both leaders and laymen who want to follow God's plan for their life and to achieve maximum results.

Pastor Denny Beavers, Living Word Church, Jonesboro, Arkansas
Arkansas District Director, Rhema Ministerial Association

Lois' teaching on the local Church is some of the best I have ever heard. Lois takes us to a higher degree of understanding the local Church. This is a must-read for every Minister and also those in the Body of Christ who truly want to be all that God created them to be.

Pastor Trey Hill, The Word Fellowship Church, Kenedy, Texas

Lois has drawn from her rich experience as a minister and missionary for many years to present time-tested and Bible-based principles in her book on the church. Her teachings and insights have been a great inspiration and help to many pastors and leaders here in France. I believe her book will be used by God to bring understanding on the purpose of the church and will give fresh life to many churches, Pastors and Christian leaders all over the world. I recommend her book with enthusiasm!

Pastor Bong Burgarin, Paris, France

We first heard Lois teach on the local church at Shekinah Glory's Minister's Conference in Paris, France, and knew it was the life-changing message that the church needs to hear today. The teaching is sound, full of revelation and vital for every believer today.

Pastor Lance and Janice Fricke, Triumphant Christian Center,
Independence, Iowa